UNDER THE TABLE

ALSO BY KEVIN C. FITZPATRICK:

A Journey into Dorothy Parker's New York

AS EDITOR
Dorothy Parker: Complete Broadway 1918–1923

*The Lost Algonquin Round Table: Humor,
Fiction, Journalism, Criticism, and Poetry from
America's Most Famous Literary Circle*

UNDER THE TABLE

=== A ===

DOROTHY PARKER
Cocktail Guide

KEVIN C. FITZPATRICK

with a foreword by Allen Katz

LYONS PRESS
GUILFORD, CONNECTICUT
AN IMPRINT OF GLOBE PEQUOT PRESS

Lyons Press is an imprint of Globe Pequot Press.

Project editor: Meredith Dias
Text design: Sheryl P. Kober
Layout: Lisa Reneson

Library of Congress Cataloging-in-Publication Data

Fitzpatrick, Kevin C., 1966-
Under the table : a Dorothy Parker cocktail guide / Kevin C. Fitzpatrick.
pages cm
ISBN 978-0-7627-9268-9 (hardback)
1. Cocktails—United States. 2. Parker, Dorothy, 1893-1967. 3. United States—Social life and customs—1918-1945. I. Title. II. Title: Dorothy Parker cocktail guide.
TX951.F53 2013
641.87'4—dc23

2013024383

Printed in the United States of America

10 9 8 7 6 5 4 3 2 1

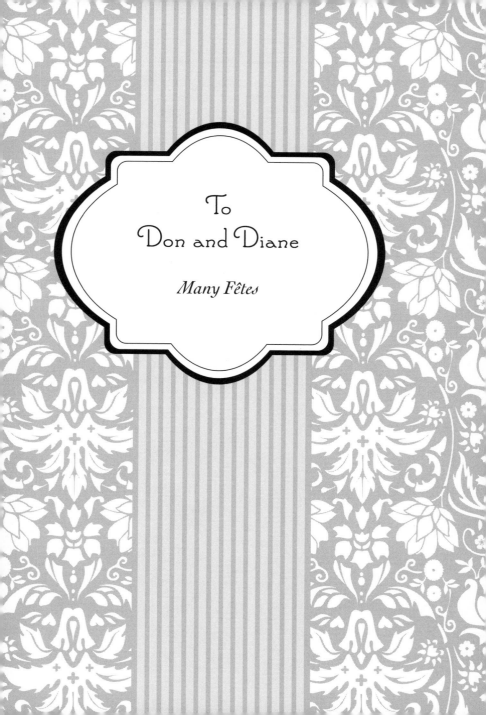

To
Don and Diane

Many Fêtes

———— ♦ ♦ ♦ ————

I love a martini—

But two at the most.

Three, I'm under the table;

Four, I'm under the host.

———— ♦ ♦ ♦ ————

Contents

Foreword

I WAS INTRODUCED TO THE ACERBIC WIT OF DOROTHY PARKER IN COLLEGE. Studying the lyrics of Tin Pan Alley, I came across the elegant patter of Cole Porter. "As Dorothy Parker once said" immediately piqued my curiosity. Of the musical numbers from 1935's *Jubilee*, I would sooner take "Begin the Beguine," but of all the characters in "Just One of Those Things" only Juliet and Romeo were familiar to me. In those days, before the dawn of the Internet age, there was no Google search, so I hit the stacks and came upon *The Collected Poetry of Dorothy Parker*. "Ballade of a Talked-Off Ear" still stands out.

By the time I graduated—*Dorothy Parker Stories* a fitting commencement gift—I was on my way to New York to seek fame and fortune. I didn't know at the time that a future in drinks and the wonderfully fitting American culture of cocktails awaited me, but in short time, absorbed by the rush of history and the pleasure of a well-made Manhattan, suddenly her name appeared again: Dorothy Parker and the Algonquin Round Table. The Round Table itself, long before *Mad Men*, provided an interesting social concept: literati and the three-martini lunch. Instantly I was less interested in the hard talking and more interested in the hard drinking!

Dorothy Parker came of age in an era when men and women in urban America didn't socialize at bars. The saloons of the pre-Prohibition era offered taps for men of varied walks of life to blow off steam, share a story or two, and imbibe. Once in a while an establishment might have a side door or a ladies' entrance, but the idea of a woman lunching and drinking with men in a professional scenario was sadly a rarity. Parker helped change that, contributing, if you will, to the democratization of drinking culture—and what more democratic place should there be than a bar?

In a time of restless brilliance, her national celebrity sprang from the sharp, biting humor of both her incisive poetry and her widely quoted quips. Regularly seated at the famed Algonquin Round Table, she took center stage in the city's cultural and intellectual beating heart. No one could have been a more interesting drinking companion, and our Dorothy Parker American Gin celebrates her unconventionality in all its glittering facets.

Under the Table gives us a glance at a bygone era and at Dorothy Parker herself: drinker, for certain, but writer, raconteuse, and provocateuse as well. Not just a reminiscence, it acknowledges a rejuvenation of cocktail culture, the importance of patience and the art of conversation, and the myriad rewards of a well-made drink.

—Allen Katz
Cofounder of the New York Distilling Company

Introduction

STIRRING THE LIFE OF DOROTHY PARKER

NO OTHER AMERICAN WRITER HAS A REPUTATION QUITE LIKE THE ONE DOROTHY Parker earned. Almost fifty years after her death, her numerous wisecracks live on, such as her advice to a friend who needed to euthanize an old cat: "Try curiosity." Or about a boyfriend: "His voice was as intimate as the rustle of sheets." After she learned that President Coolidge had died, she remarked: "How can you tell?"

But Mrs. Parker did more than crack wise and create bad puns. The American Academy of Arts and Letters admitted her to its ranks not for telling jokes but for the achievements of her poetry and short stories. She went into the New York Writers Hall of Fame alongside Herman Melville and Willa Cather. Not a day goes by that her name doesn't pop up on the Internet, in the umpteenth pop culture reference of the day's news cycle.

She's also renowned for writing about booze, talking about drinking, and loving a cocktail or two herself. Along with her dogs and expensive clothes, Mrs. Parker also enjoyed her cocktails. She imbibed at speakeasies in New York, mansions in Beverly Hills, and villas on the French Riviera. A friend once said, "You've got to expect public recognition like that. After all, you're an international celebrity." To which Mrs. Parker replied, "Yeah, that's me, the toast of two continents—Greenland and Australia."

◆ ◆ ◆

Dorothy was born to New Yorkers J. Henry and Elizabeth (née Marston) Rothschild on August 22, 1893, at their summer beach cottage in Long Branch, New Jersey, near present-day 732 Ocean Avenue, facing the beach. Her father worked in the garment business, making men's cloaks and suits. The comfortably upper–middle class family had housekeepers and cooks but weren't considered wealthy.

When Dorothy Parker walked into a kitchen one morning, her host asked what he could make for her breakfast. "Just something light and easy to fix," she said. "How about a dear little whiskey sour?"

Her childhood on Manhattan's Upper West Side was an unhappy one. Young Dorothy attended a Catholic grammar school, then a finishing school in Morristown, New Jersey. Her formal education ended abruptly at age fourteen. A voracious reader, she often wrote poems for her father. Both her mother and stepmother died when she was young; her uncle, Martin Rothschild, perished on the *Titanic* in 1912, and her father died the following year.

In 1914 Mrs. Parker sold her first poem to *Vanity Fair*. At age twenty-one, she took an editorial job at *Vogue*. She couldn't believe how overdecorated the offices were, though. "Well, it looks just like the entrance to a house of ill-fame," she remarked later. She continued writing poems for newspapers and magazines, and in 1917 she joined *Vanity Fair*, taking over for P. G. Wodehouse as drama critic—making her the first female critic on Broadway. That same year, she married stockbroker

Dorothy Parker
in the 1920s ◆ ◆ ◆

Edwin Pond Parker II. The marriage proved tempestuous, though, and the couple divorced in 1928.

In 1919 Mrs. Parker became a founding member of the Algonquin Round Table, an informal gathering of writers who lunched at the Algonquin Hotel in Midtown Manhattan. The "Vicious Circle"—which was the nickname of the group rather than the piece of furniture around which they gathered—included Alexander Woollcott, Robert Benchley, Harpo Marx, George S. Kaufman, and Edna Ferber and earned a reputation for its scathing wit and intellectual commentary. In 1922, *Smart Set* published Mrs. Parker's first short story, "Such a Pretty Little Picture."

One year after ratification of the Eighteenth Amendment outlawed the manufacture and sale of alcohol, National Prohibition went into practice in January 1920. Mrs. Parker was twenty-six. She and her friends frequented the local speakeasies, particularly on West Forty-ninth Street, where Rockefeller Center stands today. There was no drinking at the Algonquin Hotel, however. General manager Frank Case took the bar out during World War I, keeping the restaurant in operation by serving tea and coffee. The Vicious Circle luncheons were "dry" affairs.

When *The New Yorker* debuted in 1925, Mrs. Parker was listed on the editorial board. Over the years, she contributed poetry, fiction, theater criticism, and book reviews as "Constant Reader." Her first collection of poetry, *Enough Rope*, appeared in 1926 and became a best seller. Her two subsequent collections were *Sunset Gun* in 1928 and *Death and Taxes* in 1931. Her collected fiction came out in 1930 as *Laments for the Living*.

Reviews were good, and her popularity swelled. Mrs. Parker traveled to Europe several times, befriending Ernest Hemingway, Scott and Zelda Fitzgerald, and socialites Gerald and Sara Murphy, among others. In the 1920s she contributed articles to *The New Yorker* and *Life*. While her work garnered her success and regard for her wit and conversational abilities, she suffered from depression and alcoholism and attempted suicide.

In 1929 Mrs. Parker won the O. Henry Award for her semi-autobiographical short story "Big Blonde." She wrote short fiction in the early 1930s, and in 1931 she returned to her role as a Broadway critic, subbing for

Robert Benchley for several issues of *The New Yorker* while he was in California. She delivered a particularly stinging put-down to a Channing Pollock drama: "I may mutter only that *The House Beautiful* is, for me, the play lousy."

In 1934 Mrs. Parker married actor-writer Alan Campbell in New Mexico. The bride was forty; the groom twenty-nine. The couple relocated to Los Angeles and became a highly paid screenwriting team. They labored for MGM and Paramount on mostly forgettable features. Of the nearly forty screenplays that Mrs. Parker worked on, only a handful are available today on DVD. The highlight of her film career was an Academy Award nomination for *A Star Is Born* in 1937. The couple divorced in 1947 and remarried in 1950.

Mrs. Parker was inducted into the American Academy of Arts and Letters in 1959. Following her husband's death in 1963, Dorothy returned to New York City. On June 6, 1967, she was found in her Upper East Side apartment, dead of a heart attack at age seventy-three. A firm believer in civil rights, she bequeathed her literary estate to Martin Luther King Jr. On his assassination, less than a year later, the estate was turned over to the National Association for the Advancement of Colored People (NAACP). Her remains were cremated and her ashes interred in a memorial garden at the NAACP headquarters in Baltimore, Maryland.

Within twenty of years of her death, three biographies appeared, which opened the taps for a new generation to discover Dorothy Parker. In the 1990s her short fiction and poetry were collected in new editions and became steady sellers. Mrs. Parker's work was translated into French, Spanish, Portuguese, and Russian. For the centennial of her birth, a commemorative postage stamp was dedicated not far from where she was born on the Jersey Shore. The 1994 feature film *Mrs. Parker and the Vicious Circle*, directed by Alan Rudolph and featuring an all-star cast, with Jennifer Jason Leigh in the lead role, was a critical success. In 1999 the Dorothy Parker Society (DorothyParker.com) was launched to promote the work of and introduce new readers to Dorothy Parker (and have as much fun as possible). Today the society has more than five thousand members worldwide. As the fiftieth anniversary of Mrs. Parker's death approaches, more of her poems, fiction, and essays are available now than when she was alive, and her reputation as one of America's most original voices is solidly established.

Cocktails 101

This is a quick overview of basic bartending equipment, a glassware glossary of basic cocktail glasses, and some key mixing tips and tricks.

Equipment for the Bartender

You can find the essential equipment for preparing these recipes in a home goods shop, restaurant supply store, or online auctions for vintage bar tools. Part of the lure of mixing cocktails derives from the paraphernalia and equipment needed. Just locating a vintage cocktail shaker and bar spoon will put you in the mood to start mixing drinks. These are the top pieces of essential bar equipment:

bar spoon: Many drinks require the use of a long-handled flat-head spoon. Find one with a twisted shaft if possible, which feels better when stirring a drink.

channel knife: A lemon peel is cut into long spirals using this sharp, small knife. It is a flat piece of steel with an opening to cut the peel evenly.

chef's knife: Best used for slicing large fruit such as lemons and limes. Keep it with a small cutting board.

cocktail shaker: This is the most important tool you'll need to make a cocktail. Heavy stainless steel cocktail shakers guarantee the coldest drinks. Hunt around for antique sterling silver models of the "silver bullet" variety. The cocktail shaker will serve your needs for both shaking and stirring mixed drinks.

cocktail shaker, Boston: The bottom half of a Boston cocktail shaker is stainless steel, and the top is made of glass. It also doubles as a mixing glass.

cocktail strainer: Also called a Hawthorne or Lindley strainer, this has coils around the sides and is placed over the cocktail shaker.

corkscrew: You can choose from various models, but look for a vintage waiter's style corkscrew with a folding knife attachment (all the better for cutting foil and labels around the necks of bottles). The modern rabbit type with a lever pull is excellent, but the cheap ones quickly wear out with regular use.

dishware: A few nice porcelain or china pieces are perfect for placing olives, limes, and garnishes on the bar. Conversely, obtain some good plastic containers in which to store your perishables overnight.

ice bucket and tongs: Keep your ice cubes handy in a bucket. Long tongs to grab ice cubes are more classy than a spoon (or your fingers).

ice spoon: Also known as a julep strainer, this spoon is semi-flat with holes in it and is placed over the cocktail shaker.

jiggers and shot glasses: These are indispensable for measuring that perfect drink. Some 2-ounce jiggers have markings for 1½, 1, and ½ ounces. Shot glasses can come in these sizes as well.

juicer or reamer: A juicer or reamer has holes to catch the seeds and pulp of fresh fruit. Use a bowl to collect the juice.

measuring cups and spoons: Just like a kitchen set, measuring cups from ½ cup on up. A set that has tablespoons and teaspoons as well is key.

muddler: This is a rod, similar to a pestle, used for crushing or "muddling" fruit. It has a broad, rounded, or flat end. Get a wooden one because it won't scratch glass. You cannot make a Mint Julep without a muddler.

opener: Many recipes require juices and mixes that require a bottle or can opener.

paring knife: All bars need this indispensable knife. It should be 4 inches long and thin and have a spear tip. Keep it sharpened.

pitcher: Find a beautiful glass pitcher and use it for all stirred cocktails. It will look impressive when filled with ice cubes while also delivering drinks properly chilled.

Glassware

Not all glassware was created for the same purpose. You don't serve a Sidecar in a beer mug. A short list follows from among the two dozen or more types of bar glasses. It ignores the whole army of wine glasses and goblets and instead sticks to the glasses you will need to make the drinks in this guidebook. All cocktails are served in these basic types of glassware. Thinking about using a plastic cup? You should be ashamed.

champagne (4 to 10 ounces): The expected glass to serve Champagne is tall and graceful, also called a *tulip* and a *flute*. The reason for its shape? The smaller surface allows fewer bubbles to escape.

cocktail (3 to 10 ounces): This is the classic stemmed glass for drinks served without ice. For larger drinks the bowls have become wider. Also called a *martini glass*.

Collins (10 to 14 ounces): Slimmer and taller than a highball glass, the name of this glass derives from the Collins family of drinks.

coupe (5 to 10 ounces): Traditionally a small round bowl on a long stem—often used for Champagne—this glass is shallower than a wine goblet. The French claim it was modeled in the shape of Marie Antoinette's left breast. It's back in vogue for cocktails that don't require ice because the long stem prevents body heat from transferring to the drink. It's utterly classic.

highball (8 to 12 ounces): This is the most common bar glass for drinks with ice cubes. A **lowball** is half this size.

Nick & Nora (6 to 8 ounces): A smallish glass with a modest stem, this classic shape has a cult following that insists it's the best glass for serving Martinis. It takes its name from a pair of cocktail-loving gumshoes created by Dashiell Hammett; Nick and Nora Charles first appeared in his 1934 detective novel, *The Thin Man*. Other writers transferred the couple to radio, motion pictures, television, and Broadway shows. It's perfect for any cocktail served straight up.

old-fashioned (4 to 8 ounces): It takes its name from the eponymous cocktail and is usually a short, squat glass used for drinks with ice. Also called a *rocks glass* or *whiskey glass*.

sour (5 to 6 ounces): Used for sours and juice drinks of all kinds. Also called *whiskey sour glass, Rickey glass, fizz glass,* or a *Delmonico,* after the old New York restaurant.

Wine (4 to 8 ounces): From goblets to Reidel, each shape is for a different relationship between volume and surface area. Tapered bowls are designed for the free circulation of the wine to allow the vapors to "breathe" more.

Mixing Tips and Tricks

◆ There isn't a cocktail in this book that doesn't have one key ingredient: ice. In the old days bartenders took blocks of ice and cut off pieces to suit the drink. In our more modern age, ice is more plentiful, and you can use more of it. (Don't ever reuse ice cubes from one cocktail shaker to the next, though; never use the same ice twice!) If a recipe calls for "cracked" or "shaved" ice, take a good amount of cubed ice and wrap it in a clean, dry bar towel. Then, using a wooden mallet or heavy spoon, beat the heck out of it and drop the ice into the cocktail shaker. For drinks that are shaken, use cracked ice. The longer you shake it, the colder the drink.

◆ Cocktail shakers and mixing glasses are essential to superb cocktails. In his book, *Imbibe!*, bartender historian David Wondrich clarifies when to shake and when to stir: "Modern orthodoxy dictates that one should shake any drink with fruit juices, dairy products, or eggs and stir ones that contain only spirits, wines, and the like. This is based partly on the fact that shaking clouds up liquids by beating thousands of tiny bubbles into them." Cloudy drinks come from the shaking, which is why a Manhattan or Martini that's crystal clear is stirred, not shaken. A muddler requires a lot of work, but the effort of mashing the ingredients between your palm and a wooden stick are worth it when making your concoctions by hand.

◆ When straining a drink made in a mixing glass or cocktail shaker, keep the ice out of the glass by holding a cocktail strainer or julep strainer over the top of the shaker or mixing glass. Carefully pour the drink into the glass, and the ice won't fall in.

- If a recipe calls for a float, this means pouring one liquid atop another. To do this, pour the first spirit in the glass. Then, hover a bar spoon upside down just over the surface of the drink. Pour the second, floated spirit slowly over the back of the spoon so it drips on top of the first.

- Cold cocktails? Of course. Always use chilled glassware. Store them in a refrigerator or freezer for at least an hour before use. Another trick is the "flash chill," which means filling them with crushed ice for 15 minutes. Always handle the glasses by the stem or bottom, not the sides, so your body heat doesn't transfer to the drink. Always serve mixers such as soda and fruit juice cold. Never pour them warm from a bottle or can.

- Finally, make it and serve it. Your cocktails have to be served immediately to be any good. London bartender god Harry Craddock was once asked the best way to drink a cocktail: "*Quickly,*" he replied, "while it's laughing at you!"

- Use this book as a manual to plan your own speakeasy parties or to serve vintage drinks at your bar.

THE DRINKS

In 1928 fellow poet William Rose Benét wrote: "What the devil can you do with such a girl? You can be moved to sympathy by some expression of evident distress, or to admiration for some gallantry of attitude, or to gravity at an occasional tenderness—and then she flips a last line at you like a little carmine firecracker exploding under your nose. And it is all Dorothy Parker."

The Acerbic Mrs. Parker

The Shanty, Brooklyn

NO SHORTAGE OF BARTENDERS WANTS TO HONOR MRS. PARKER WITH A NAMESAKE cocktail. Countless recipes have been created and named for her around the globe, from the Algonquin Hotel to a popular discothèque named Club Dorothy Parker in Rio de Janeiro. This one came to life in Brooklyn, created by Allen Katz, general manager of the New York Distilling Company. *The Portable Dorothy Parker,* which he picked up in college, instantly had him hooked. At their wedding, he and his wife exchanged vows and read "Here We Are" to each other. Katz pressed his business partners to launch Dorothy Parker American Gin as one of the company's first brands. He created the Acerbic Mrs. Parker in the Shanty, the little bar next to their Brooklyn distilling operation.

collins glass

2 ounces Dorothy Parker American Gin
¼ ounce Combier orange liqueur
½ ounce hibiscus syrup
½ ounce fresh lemon juice
Seltzer
Lemon twist

SHAKE ALL LIQUID INGREDIENTS EXCEPT THE SELTZER OVER ICE; STRAIN
INTO A COLLINS GLASS FILLED WITH FRESH ICE. TOP WITH CHILLED SELTZER
AND GARNISH WITH A LEMON TWIST. SERVE WITH A STRAW.

Alexander

THE ALGONQUIN ROUND TABLE MET FOR THE FIRST TIME IN JUNE 1919 TO WELCOME Alexander Woollcott back to New York after serving in the army for two years. The rotund *Times* critic and Dorothy Parker shared the distinction of being born on the New Jersey Shore. Woollcott famously said, "All the things I really like to do are either immoral, illegal, or fattening." In 1922 he took up residence in a Hell's Kitchen townhouse with one of the married couples of the Vicious Circle, editor Harold Ross and journalist Jane Grant. Mrs. Parker named their house Wit's End. When Woollcott moved out a few years later, he took with him the housekeeper, his family's silver, and the house's nickname. He always claimed the Brandy Alexander was named for him, but that was a fib. This recipe comes from bartender Hugo R. Ensslin's 1916 collection *Recipes for Mixed Drinks*.

cocktail glass

1½ ounces Crème de Cacao
1½ ounces brandy
1½ ounces fresh cream

SHAKE ALL INGREDIENTS OVER ICE; STRAIN INTO A COCKTAIL GLASS.

Alexander Woolcott called Dorothy Parker "a blend of Little Nell and Lady Macbeth." ◆ ◆ ◆

Algonquin Cocktail

LONG BEFORE THE VICIOUS CIRCLE BEGAN MEETING AROUND THE ALGONQUIN Round Table, the hotel, located at 59 West Forty-fourth Street, had a reputation for attracting actors and writers. Upstate gambler Albert T. Foster began the enterprise, the first guests checking in on November 22, 1902. A standard room and bath cost two dollars a day, while a three-bedroom, three-bath suite with private hall, sitting room, dining room, and library ran ten dollars. The best move Foster made was hiring Frank Case as general manager. Case ran a tight ship and ran the hotel for twenty-five years before buying it. News of the sale ran on the front page of the *New York Times*. The hotel has changed hands a half a dozen times over the last century, but its history and traditions remain. There are several variations of the Algonquin Cocktail, but this is how the bartenders mix them in the hotel's elegant Blue Bar.

cocktail glass

old-fashioned glass

1½ ounces rye whiskey
¾ ounce dry vermouth
¾ ounce pineapple juice (unsweetened)
Maraschino cherry

STIR THE RYE WHISKEY, VERMOUTH, AND JUICE IN A COCKTAIL SHAKER
FILLED WITH ICE. STRAIN INTO A CHILLED COCKTAIL GLASS OR OVER ICE
INTO AN OLD-FASHIONED GLASS. GARNISH WITH THE CHERRY.

◆ ◆ ◆

"I bought the Algonquin because I love it and the associations that go with it and the people who have helped me by their patronage to make it what it is," said Frank Case in 1927. In an era when actors and actresses were considered little more than and treated little better than prostitutes, Case warmly welcomed theater folk. He also attracted writers and editors from the nearby publishing offices of city newspapers and magazines, including Parker and the Vicious Circle.

The Round Table Room in the Algonquin Hotel ◆ ◆ ◆

Angel's Tit

DOROTHY PARKER WAS NO ANGEL, AND SHE REVELED IN IT. WHEN ASKED WHY SHE preferred hotels to owning a house, she replied that all she needed was "room enough to lay a hat and a few friends." While she was living at the Algonquin Hotel, general manager Frank Case suspected her of breaking a house rule and telephoned her suite.

"Do you have a gentleman in your room?" he inquired.

"Just a minute," Mrs. Parker answered. "I'll ask him."

During the 1920s, this popular after-dinner drink proved a delight to order and to imbibe. Its naughty name derives from the placement of the garnish.

cocktail glass

1½ ounces maraschino liqueur
¾ ounce fresh cream
Maraschino cherry

POUR THE MARASCHINO LIQUEUR, SUCH AS MARASKA OR LUXARDO, INTO A CHILLED COCKTAIL GLASS. FLOAT THE CREAM ON TOP. THE CHERRY GARNISH MUST BE PERFECTLY PLACED ON TOP, AND IN THE CENTER, FOR THE FULL EFFECT. ALTERNATELY YOU CAN USE EQUAL PARTS LIQUEUR AND CREAM, WHIPPING IT INTO A SCULPTED FROTH—BUT THAT'S A LOT OF WORK.

— ◆ ◆ ◆ —

The play rather pines away later on, however; there are long stretches when the only thing that rivets your attention to the stage is wondering at what moment the shoulder straps of Julia Bruns' green gown are going to give up the unequal struggle and succumb to the strain."

—Mrs. Parker's review of *The Blue Pearl* in
Vanity Fair, October 1918

Auntie Jo-Jo's Jalapeño Bloody Maria

Doc Holliday's Saloon, New York City

THE MARTINI AND BLOODY MARY VIE FOR THE TITLE OF MOST POPULAR COCKTAIL IN America. If the Martini lubricates sophisticated Friday evening conversations, the Bloody Mary colludes with your Saturday morning steak and eggs. Legend has it that barman Pete Petiot of Harry's New York Bar in Paris created the concoction around 1921. When Prohibition ended, the Hotel St. Regis lured him to Manhattan, and by World War II the Bloody Mary was everywhere. Nearly a century later the drink has transformed as often as the city itself.

On a noisy corner in Manhattan's East Village lies Doc Holliday's, a neighborhood shot-and-beer joint. Facing Tompkins Square Park on Avenue A, Doc's serves oceans of the hard stuff, its clientele preferring tequila, whiskey, and vodka. For twenty years Joanna Leban has wielded the stick at Doc's. A savvy poker player, witty raconteuse, and an encyclopedia of drinks, she developed this variation on the drink, serving it on weekend brunch shifts.

pint glass

Makes six 16-ounce servings

3 cups tomato juice
2 jalapeños, seeded and finely chopped
1 tablespoon freshly grated horseradish
Juice of 1 lemon
Juice of 1 lime
1 teaspoon original Cholula hot sauce
Splash of balsamic vinegar
¼ teaspoon salt (more to taste)
¼ teaspoon Cajun spice
1 cup Tanteo jalapeño-infused tequila

3 jalapeño-stuffed olives
1 celery stalk
3 pickled Cajun green beans
1 lime wedge

TO MAKE THE BLOODY MARIA MIX, COMBINE THE TOMATO JUICE, JALAPEÑOS, HORSERADISH, LEMON AND LIME JUICES, HOT SAUCE, AND VINEGAR. IN A SEPARATE CONTAINER, COMBINE THE SALT AND CAJUN SPICE; RIM GLASS WITH THE MIXTURE. COMBINE THE BLOODY MARIA MIX AND TEQUILA AND POUR OVER ICE INTO RIMMED PINT GLASSES. SPLIT CELERY STALK LENGTHWISE, PLACE HALVES OFF CENTER INSIDE GLASSES. GARNISH WITH OLIVES SPIKED ON A MIXING STICK. ADD PICKLED BEANS AS A GARNISH, AND ADD LIME WEDGE TO THE RIM.

Note: Joanna's Jalapeño Bloody Maria is so popular that she makes them six at a time. If you can't find jalapeño-infused tequila, substitute a good silver tequila. You may also substitute jarred horseradish if you can't find fresh. For a twist, try Effen cucumber vodka, and you get Auntie Jo-Jo's Jalapeño Cool as a Cucumber Bloody Maria.

◆ ◆ ◆

What makes a bartender great? The ability to adapt to each customer's needs. It's all strategy. It's like poker: "Play the player, not the game." When a customer asks what time it is, I tell him, "It's time to drink." Being a bartender is like hosting a party every night.
—Joanna Leban, East Village, New York City

Aviation

DURING THE HUDSON-FULTON CELEBRATION IN 1909, THOUSANDS CHEERED AS Wilbur Wright made two round-trip flights from Governors Island in New York Harbor, one around the Statue of Liberty and the second up the Hudson River to Grant's Tomb and back. When Charles Lindbergh returned to New York after his historic solo flight to Paris in 1927, a crowd of four million attended his tickertape parade on Broadway. In 1932 Amelia Earhart returned from her own transatlantic flight an instant national icon. The Aviation cocktail captures the flying spirit of the era. It was a favorite at the Hotel Wallick, a landmark 400-room Times Square hotel on the corner of Broadway and Forty-third Street. The hotel's manager, German-born Hugo R. Ensslin, had the foresight to collect his favorite cocktail recipes before Prohibition began. Published in 1916, *Recipes for Mixed Drinks* made the Aviation take off.

cocktail glass

1½ ounces gin
1 teaspoon maraschino liqueur
1 teaspoon Crème de Violette
Juice of 1 lemon

IN A COCKTAIL SHAKER, POUR ALL THE INGREDIENTS OVER CRACKED ICE.
SHAKE AND STRAIN INTO A CHILLED COCKTAIL GLASS.

Note: The Crème de Violette is the key but often-missing ingredient that
also nicely turns the drink a sky-blue color. Use just a little.

Bailey

DOROTHY PARKER COUNTED GERALD AND SARA MURPHY AMONG HER DEAREST friends, but she wasn't the only one. Jazz Age artists and literati from Dos Passos to Picasso enjoyed the company of the American expatriate couple. Their Cap d'Antibes house, Villa America, hosted legendary parties when they lived in France from 1921 to 1929, and the couple inspired the characters Dick and Nicole Diver in F. Scott Fitzgerald's *Tender Is the Night*. Mrs. Parker lived with them for six months in Switzerland when their young son was fighting tuberculosis. "Sara is in love with life and skeptical of people," said Gerald Murphy, a gifted painter and writer. "I'm the other way. I believe you have to do things to life to make it tolerable. I've always liked the old Spanish proverb: 'Living well is the best revenge.'" To that end, Gerald's drink-mixing skills proved formidable. Using gin, he created what he called a Bailey: "invented by me," he wrote to Alexander Woollcott, "as were a great many other good things." Mrs. Parker remained lifelong friends with the couple, and, when she returned home to Manhattan from Los Angeles in 1963, she moved into Sara Murphy's apartment building on the Upper East Side.

cocktail glass

Mint sprigs
1½ ounces gin
½ ounce fresh grapefruit juice
½ ounce fresh lime juice

GERALD MURPHY'S INSTRUCTIONS: "THE MINT SHOULD BE PUT IN THE SHAKER FIRST. IT SHOULD BE TORN UP BY HAND AS IT STEEPS BETTER. THE GIN SHOULD BE ADDED THEN AND ALLOWED TO STAND A MINUTE OR TWO. THEN ADD THE GRAPEFRUIT JUICE AND THEN THE LIME JUICE. STIR VIGOROUSLY WITH ICE AND DO NOT ALLOW TO DILUTE TOO MUCH, BUT SERVE VERY COLD, WITH A SPRIG OF MINT IN EACH GLASS."

Bathtub Gin

Jane Grant's recipe

ONE OF THE FORGOTTEN STARS OF THE JAZZ AGE, ROUND TABLE MEMBER JANE Grant cofounded *The New Yorker* with her husband, Harold Ross, at their kitchen table at 412 West Forty-seventh Street in 1925. The Hell's Kitchen townhouse still stands, once the scene of raucous parties attended by the Vicious Circle, Ethel Barrymore, Irving Berlin, F. Scott Fitzgerald, and others. But those parties put Grant in a fix because her guests required more alcohol than her bootleggers could provide. She started distilling her own gin from a recipe that she claimed came from the maître d'hôtel at the old Waldorf-Astoria Hotel. ("If the Waldorf could fool the customers, I could impress my friends, and I would not be exposing them to a fate worse than death.") But first she needed pure alcohol. "I finally found a reliable bootlegger who would deliver it in ten-gallon cans—nothing less. At first that was a little staggering. My recipe called for equal parts water—and twenty gallons of gin seemed like a lot of gin to me . . . My supply was consumed with true speakeasy gusto—I soon found that twenty gallons of gin was not an extravagant amount for 412."

1 quart pure grain alcohol
8 drops oil of juniper
1 to 1¼ quart distilled water

MIX ALCOHOL AND OIL WELL SEVERAL TIMES FOR 30 TO 36 HOURS, THEN
ADD THE DISTILLED WATER. MIX WELL FOR 20 TO 24 HOURS.

Note: Grant recommended shaking the bottles every day for a week, much to the chagrin of her friends. "Not one of the wretches would give me a hand, preferring, as they said, sudden blindness, or even death, to such labor . . . Everyone else, they pointed out, just mixed the ingredients and served—I was much too fussy."

Bathtub Gin in Chelsea—which serves many of the drinks in this book—creates a fun simulacrum of a speakeasy experience with the Stone Street Coffeehouse exterior. Bathtub Gin has been adopted as the name of modern speakeasies located today in New York City, Seattle, and Mooresville, North Carolina.

The birthplace of *The New Yorker* was on the second floor of this Hell's Kitchen townhouse. ◆ ◆ ◆

Between the Sheets

Dorothy Parker and Alan Campbell divorced in 1947, ending twelve rocky years of marriage. Both took up with others almost immediately, but the two were so codependent that they reunited three years later. One wag said of Campbell, "He was sweet-tempered when sober, with an endearing sort of wanting to be helpful. He was Dorothy Parker's *helpmate* in nearly every sense of the word." They remarried in a splashy Beverly Hills ceremony in 1950. On the morning of their second wedding day, Dorothy and Alan lay in bed together. She pulled the sheet over her face. "No peeking," she said. "Mustn't see the bride before the wedding!" The Between the Sheets cocktail dates to the 1920s in two competing recipes. The first version comes from the 1937 *Café Royal Cocktail Book*, published in London, with two competing liquors as the base.

cocktail glass

1 ounce brandy
1 ounce rum
1 ounce Cointreau
1 dash lemon juice

SHAKE ALL INGREDIENTS OVER ICE AND STRAIN INTO A CHILLED COCKTAIL GLASS.

Note: Use a premium white rum for best result. You can substitute the brandy with Cognac.

The second recipe comes from Havana, where this 1935 Cuban version from Bar La Florida tastes sweeter but just as delicious.

cocktail glass

1 ounce Cognac
1 ounce Crème de Cacao
1 ounce sweet cream or half-and-half
1 dash Angostura bitters
1 teaspoon sugar
Lemon peel

SHAKE ALL INGREDIENTS EXCEPT LEMON PEEL OVER PLENTY OF CRACKED ICE; STRAIN INTO A CHILLED COCKTAIL GLASS. GARNISH WITH LEMON PEEL.

The second wedding of Dorothy Parker and Alan Campbell took place in 1950. ◆ ◆ ◆

Blood and Sand

"I HATE HUSBANDS; THEY NARROW MY SCOPE," DOROTHY PARKER WROTE IN ONE OF her notorious "Hymns of Hate," adding:

There are the Home Bodies;
They are seldom mistaken for Rudolph Valentino;
The militia has not yet been called out to keep the women back.

One of the first drinks to come out of Hollywood was the Blood and Sand, named for the 1922 Rudolph Valentino film of the same title. The biggest film celebrity of the decade, Valentino died in 1927 in New York, aged just 31. Two female fans tried to commit suicide in front of his hospital, and more than 100,000 people thronged the streets around Frank Campbell's Funeral Chapel during his wake. Harry Craddock served this drink at the Savoy Hotel in London during the 1920s.

cocktail glass

¾ ounce Scotch
¾ ounce cherry brandy
¾ ounce sweet vermouth
¾ ounce orange juice

SHAKE ALL INGREDIENTS OVER CRACKED ICE; STRAIN INTO A CHILLED COCKTAIL GLASS.

Valentino and Dorothy Parker had something in common: Both of their memorial services took place at Frank Campbell's funeral home. ◆ ◆ ◆

Boulevard

THE 1940 US CENSUS FOUND DOROTHY PARKER LIVING NEXT TO ROBERT BENCHLEY on Sunset Boulevard in West Hollywood at the Garden of Allah, a collection of tiny villas grouped around a swimming pool. The bungalow rentals proved popular with movie and radio celebrities because the development was affordable, semiprivate, and a short drive to the studios. Alla Nazimova, the first actress billed as a movie star, had built what became the Garden of Allah in the early 1920s as her country home. Sunset Boulevard the rural roadway quickly transformed into The Strip, and Nazimova carved the property into twenty or thirty villas. For two decades stars such as Bogart, Fitzgerald, Garbo, Hemingway, and Welles lived there. During World War II Benchley offended a man in uniform at the bar at the Garden of Allah by addressing him as a lieutenant.

"I happen to be Captain So-and-So of the US Navy," the man said haughtily, "and may I ask who you are?"

"Me?" said Benchley. "Oh, just call me a destroyer."

The Garden of Allah was demolished in 1959, and a shopping center stands in its place. The Boulevard offers a time-honored variation on a dry Manhattan.

cocktail glass

2 ounces bourbon
½ ounce dry vermouth
½ ounce Grand Marnier
2 dashes orange bitters
Orange peel

STIR ALL INGREDIENTS EXCEPT ORANGE PEEL WITH ICE; STRAIN INTO A CHILLED COCKTAIL GLASS. GARNISH WITH FLAMED ORANGE PEEL. HOLD A MATCH UNDER THE PEEL SIDE OF A QUARTER-INCH ORANGE PEEL, OVER THE DRINK. TWIST AND SQUEEZE OVER THE DRINK. RUB THE PEEL ON THE RIM OF THE GLASS AND THEN DROP IT IN.

Note: Another variation calls for substituting rye whiskey for the bourbon.

Bronx

Jane Grant and Harold Ross, cofounders of *The New Yorker*, often served this cocktail at their Hell's Kitchen townhouse in the 1920s. At the couple's housewarming party in 1922, Mrs. Parker and her boyfriend at the time, Charles MacArthur, hired ponies for the neighborhood kids. At one memorable party, Ethel Barrymore and Alexander Woollcott improvised a scene from *Romeo and Juliet* for a crowd in the backyard. The Bronx originated at the old Waldorf-Astoria Hotel, created by bartender Johnny Solon after visiting the Bronx Zoo. Apparently the animals reminded him of some of his regulars. The hotel served so many Bronx cocktails that cases of fresh oranges were delivered daily.

cocktail glass

2 ounces gin
½ ounce dry vermouth
½ ounce sweet vermouth
1 ounce fresh orange juice

SHAKE ALL INGREDIENTS WELL WITH ICE; STRAIN INTO A CHILLED COCKTAIL GLASS.

Bulldog

DOGS PLAYED STARRING ROLES IN every part of Dorothy Parker's life. They populated her stories, poems, and plays. She never *didn't* own one, taking her puppies, mutts, and strays with her everywhere. They traveled on luxury transatlantic steamships, curled under her chair at speakeasies, and perched on her lap whenever a portrait photographer came calling. Dogs figure into many of the best Mrs. Parker tall tales. At a

Dorothy Parker took her dogs everywhere, from speakeasies to Broadway playhouses. ◆ ◆ ◆

party her dog vomited on a rug. Trying to apologize to the hostess, Mrs. Parker said, "It's the company." A more famous shaggy dog story is told about the time her pet had an accident in the Beverly Hills Hotel lobby. A manager came after her: "Miss Parker! Miss Parker! Look what your dog did!" But she stared him down: "I did it." And she walked out. The Bulldog recipe comes from the oft-forgotten pre-Prohibition bartender Hugo R. Ensslin.

cocktail glass

2 ounces cherry brandy
1 ounce rum
Juice of half a lime

SHAKE ALL INGREDIENTS OVER CRACKED ICE, STRAIN, AND SERVE IN A CHILLED COCKTAIL GLASS.

Bywater Cocktail

IT'S CLAIMED THAT TENNESSEE WILLIAMS ONCE SAID: "AMERICA HAS ONLY THREE CITIES: New York, San Francisco, and New Orleans. Everywhere else is Cleveland." A cocktail mecca sits a few paces off Bourbon Street in the French Quarter, tucked inside a hundred-year-old Creole restaurant, and you don't need to take a streetcar named Desire to reach it. "On a much smaller scale, I've often thought of the neighborhoods of New Orleans like the boroughs of New York City," says Chris Hannah, bartender at Arnaud's French 75 on Rue Bienville. "I've always compared New Orleans's Bywater to Brooklyn, so, when finally able to serve the Brooklyn Cocktail to guests at my bar, after cultivating Jamie Boudreau's Amer Picon Replica, I decided to create the Bywater Cocktail following the Brooklyn's direction. Swapping an aged rum for rye whiskey and Falernum and Chartreuse for the maraschino, I came up with a balanced cocktail worthy of the Bywater neighborhood's anomalousness."

coupe glass

1¾ ounces aged rum
¾ ounce Amer Picon or Amer Picon Replica
½ ounce Chartreuse
1 teaspoon Falernum
2 dashes Peychaud's Bitters
2 dashes orange bitters
Maraschino cherry

STIR ALL LIQUID INGREDIENTS STRAIGHT UP AND GARNISH WITH A CHERRY.

Amer Picon is a bitter aperitif produced in France with a distinct orange flavor. Falernum is a sweet syrup. Peychaud's Bitters, distributed by Sazerac, dates to around 1830, created by Antoine Amédée Peychaud, a Creole apothecary in New Orleans.

Cablegram

BEFORE E-MAIL AND TEXT MESSAGES, THE WORLD COMMUNICATED ELECTRONICALLY
with telegrams and cablegrams. Telegrams were delivered via wires to be
delivered to recipients; cablegrams were transmitted internationally via
underwater cables. Dorothy Parker was a master at both. In 1923, when
Robert E. Sherwood's first wife was expecting their child, Mary Sherwood
let everyone at the Round Table and New York know she was pregnant. To
offer her congratulations on the birth of Mary's daughter, Mrs. Parker sent a
telegram: "Good work, Mary, we all knew you had it in you." She sent it collect.
To fellow Vicious Circle member Ruth Hale, spouse of Heywood Broun and
a passionate feminist: "To Ruth Broun from Dorothy Rothschild." In 1945, Mrs.
Parker sent one to her editor at Viking Press: "This is instead of telephoning
because I can't look you in the voice. I simply cannot get that thing done yet
never have done such hard night and day work never have so wanted anything
to be good and all I have is a pile of paper covered with wrong words." The
Cablegram cocktail was a hit on both sides of the Atlantic. This recipe was
collected by Harry Craddock in his 1930 *Savoy Cocktail Book*.

lowball glass

2 ounces whiskey
½ tablespoon powdered sugar
Juice of half a lemon
Ginger ale

SHAKE ALL INGREDIENTS EXCEPT GINGER ALE OVER ICE;
STRAIN INTO A LOWBALL GLASS. ADD GINGER ALE.

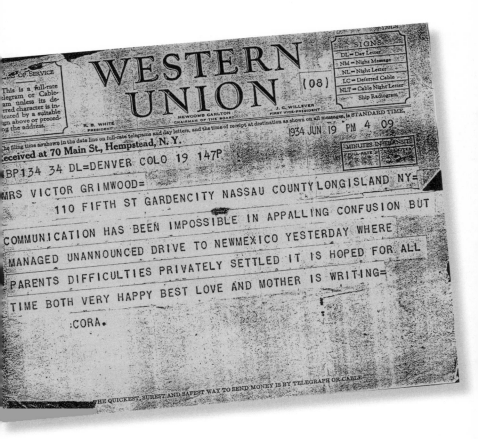

1934 JUN 19 PM 4 09

Received at 70 Main St., Hempstead, N.Y.

BP134 34 DL=DENVER COLO 19 147P

MRS VICTOR GRIMWOOD=
110 FIFTH ST GARDENCITY NASSAU COUNTY LONGISLAND NY=

COMMUNICATION HAS BEEN IMPOSSIBLE IN APPALLING CONFUSION BUT
MANAGED UNANNOUNCED DRIVE TO NEWMEXICO YESTERDAY WHERE
PARENTS DIFFICULTIES PRIVATELY SETTLED IT IS HOPED FOR ALL
TIME BOTH VERY HAPPY BEST LOVE AND MOTHER IS WRITING=

:CORA.

In 1934 Dorothy Parker sent this wedding announcement to her sister on Long Island. It's signed by one of Mrs. Parker's dogs. ◆ ◆ ◆

Chicago

THE GLUE THAT HELD THE ALGONQUIN ROUND TABLE TOGETHER WASN'T, AS YOU might think, Alexander Woollcott, the number one theater pundit in town. It was Franklin P. Adams, dean of the group and the most successful newspaper columnist of the bunch. Known by his initials F. P. A., Adams was born, raised, and educated in Chicago. He moved to Manhattan in 1904 and was extremely popular for forty years, his "Conning Tower" column required reading. He ran many of Dorothy Parker's most popular poems for no charge. She adored F. P. A. ("He raised me from a couplet."), and they coauthored a book together. F. P. A. had his glory years on the Pulitzer-owned *New York World*. "Nothing makes me so angry as to hear somebody say, 'That is too good for a newspaper; it is good enough for a magazine,'" he wrote. "I have never seen anything too good to appear in a newspaper." He generated millions of words over the course of his career, but he was known for his light verse. One Valentine's Day he wrote:

> *The ink is red,*
> *The rent is due,*
> *My hope is dead,*
> *And how are you?*

The Chicago is an old drink served in a wine glass. If you omit the Champagne it's called a Chicago Cocktail.

wine glass

1½ ounces brandy
Dash Angostura bitters
Dash triple sec
Dry Champagne

HARRY CRADDOCK'S 1930 RECIPE ADVISED: "SHAKE WELL AND STRAIN ... FROST EDGE OF GLASS WITH CASTOR SUGAR, AND FILL WITH CHAMPAGNE." THE CHICAGO IS MUCH MORE GLAMOROUS THAN THE CINCINNATI COCKTAIL, WHICH HUGO R. ENSSLIN DESCRIBED AS "HALF A GLASS OF BEER, FILL UP WITH SODA WATER, AND SERVE."

Dorothy Parker's mentor, Franklin P. Adams ◆ ◆ ◆

Prohibition and the Eighteenth Amendment

◆ ◆ ◆

It's easy now to shake our heads and crack smiles when talking about Prohibition and the Eighteenth Amendment, but the legislation enacted in 1919 destroyed businesses, wrecked lives, upended the economy, and still affects us today. The common misconception portrays glamorous flask-carrying dilettantes and hapless bootleggers running from the Keystone Kops, but, in reality, murderous thugs were delivering illegal substances to common Americans all too eager to break the law.

The Eighteenth Amendment, which prohibited the manufacture, sale, or transportation of alcoholic beverages in America proved a disastrous failure. During the thirteen years that it was on the books, it was widely ignored. National Prohibition went into effect at midnight on January 16, 1920, exactly one year after the amendment was ratified. Support for Prohibition often went hand in hand with the desire by native white Protestants to control European Catholics, Native Americans, Asian immigrants, and, especially in the South, blacks, giving police officers an excuse to arrest any of them on the pretext of intoxication. The "drys" blamed alcohol as the root cause of the nation's ills, and politicians took notice of European immigrants gathering in beer halls, becoming powerful voting blocs, and thought that by taking away these local bars they could destroy the newcomers' cohesiveness, their trade unions, and their voting power.

One of the main supporters of the dry laws, the Anti-Saloon League had its eyes on New York City for a key reason: It hoped (miraculously) that the millions of foreign visitors to the busiest city in America would see Prohibition working, return to their home countries, and preach for the banning of alcohol there as well. The powerful National Woman's Christian Temperance Union, another pillar of the movement, pushed for social

Public safety director Smedley "Duckboards" Butler chops open barrels of beer and pours them into Philadelphia's Schuylkill River in 1924. ◆ ◆ ◆

reform, citing the example of women and children afflicted by drunk ne'er-do-well husbands, and used women's new right to vote (as of August 1920) to lobby politicians to pass the amendment. The US Supreme Court allowed the Volstead Act, which implemented the Eighteenth Amendment, to stand, agreeing, five to four, that nothing in the Prohibition laws contravened the rights of the states.

In New York City the number of places to purchase liquor doubled, ironically, from 15,000 legal spots to more than 32,000 illegal ones. By the time Repeal went into effect on February 20, 1933, an estimated 1.4 billion gallons of illegal hard liquor had been sold nationally during those thirteen long years. Many of the bartenders whom Prohibition put out of work sailed for opportunities in Paris and London. Harry Craddock, who had tended bar at various luxury hotels in New York, went to London, where he had a long career at the Savoy Hotel. In 1930 he authored a cocktail guide that included many of the American recipes of the day.

As speakeasy culture grew, it attracted a new group to illegal backroom bars and basement saloons: women. According to Stanley Walker, the great city editor of the *New York Herald Tribune*:

> *Soon after 1920 great, ravening hordes of women began to discover what their less respectable sisters had known for years—that it was a lot of fun, if you liked it, to get soused. All over New York these up and coming females piled out of their hideaways, rang the bells of speakeasies, wheedled drugstores into selling them gin and rye, and even in establishments of great decorum begged their escorts for a nip from a hip flask. It was all very embarrassing.*

Landlords turned a collective and remunerative blind eye to the speaks, which had colorful names such as the Royal Box, the Jungle Room, the Club Chantee, and the Little Club. They sprang up in private homes, in walk-up apartments, and inside shuttered restaurants. Suppliers were everywhere and easy to find: Cigar shops, delicatessens, drug stores, shoeshine parlors, and even clothing stores offered bottles to thirsty customers. Women could walk into a department store looking for whiskey and gin using code names like "red stockings" and "white stockings."

The profits and success for the speakeasy trade proved lucrative. Walker recounted one underground

bar-restaurant with a menu "slightly heavy and Germanic, but it was tasty and filling." It was also an illegal speak. "Twenty-four men could belly up to the bar without undue crowding, and in 1927 and for more than two years thereafter the line was sometimes two deep. Jim's profits were staggering. In one year he cleared, after all expenses, bad checks, bribery, and charity, almost one hundred thousand dollars." That's about $1.3 million today.

Organized crime soon inched its fingers into the booze business in a major way, leading to an increase in gangster activity across city and state lines. Bloody shootouts and revenge killings splashed across the nation's front pages. News reports daily played out the crimes, stories that effectively helped end the liquor ban. Following Black Tuesday and the Stock Market Crash of 1929, many Americans organized protests and local campaigns to end the Volstead Act. A series of measures, first allowing the sale of watered-down beer and wine, led to a shift in the tide.

A three-year investigation ordered by President Herbert Hoover confirmed in 1931 that most states weren't enforcing the amendment. In 1932 Democrats officially supported its repeal. The overwhelming Democratic victory that year encouraged Congress to pass the Twenty-First Amendment, repealing the Eighteenth, on February 20, 1933. On March 22 the Volstead Act was amended to permit the sale of 3.2 percent beer and wine. Once Congress ratified the Twenty-First Amendment the following December, the Volstead Act became void.

The first legal drink served in the White House by FDR was a martini.

Cuba Libre

AUTHOR CHARLES H. BAKER WROTE IN THE GENTLEMAN'S COMPANION (1939) THAT one of the top high-society drinks of the era was the Cuba Libre, forerunner to today's Rum and Coke. The drink originated in Havana around the time of the Spanish-American War (1898), when a captain ordered a rum with Coca-Cola and a wedge of lime. As one drinks aficionado remarked, this became the world's most popular cocktail, uniting the staple liquids of two nations. One tall tale says Teddy Roosevelt and his Roughriders shouted "Por Cuba Libre!" ("Free Cuba!") as they toasted.

collins glass

1 small lime
1½ ounces Bacardi white rum
Coca-Cola

QUARTER THE LIME AND STRAIN THE JUICE INTO A COLLINS GLASS. SCRAPE THE PEEL CLEAN AND CUT INTO PIECES. ADD PEEL PIECES TO THE GLASS AND THEN ADD THE RUM. MUDDLE SO THAT THE LIQUID COATS THE SIDES OF THE GLASS. ADD ICE CUBES AND FILL WITH COCA-COLA.

Col. Theodore Roosevelt and the 1st US Volunteer Cavalry regiment atop San Juan Hill, Cuba, July 1898. ◆ ◆ ◆

Death in the Afternoon

In 1926 Dorothy Parker dropped by the office of friend Franklin P. Adams after returning from France, where she spent time with Ernest Hemingway. F. P. A. asked Mrs. Parker if she knew the novelist's age. "Well, I don't know," she replied. "You know, all writers are either twenty-nine or Thomas Hardy." Three years later she wrote the first profile of Hemingway to appear in *The New Yorker*. "People so much wanted him to be a figure out of a saga that they went to the length of providing the saga themselves," she wrote. "And a little peach it is." Hemingway's Spanish bullfighting classic *Death in the Afternoon* appeared in 1932. A few years later, a celebrity cocktail guide, *So Red the Nose*, received this contribution from the future Nobel winner.

champagne flute

1 ounce absinthe
Champagne

ACCORDING TO THE ORIGINAL RECIPE, HEMINGWAY WROTE: "POUR ONE JIGGER ABSINTHE INTO A CHAMPAGNE GLASS. ADD ICED CHAMPAGNE UNTIL IT ATTAINS THE PROPER OPALESCENT MILKINESS. DRINK THREE TO FIVE OF THESE SLOWLY."

◆ ◆ ◆

The only cure for a real hangover is death.
—Robert Benchley

Jack Dempsey started boxing professionally in 1914, calling himself "Kid Blackie." Damon Runyon nicknamed him the "Manassa Mauler" in 1916. ◆ ◆ ◆

Dempsey

IN 1921 THE COLORADO-BORN WORLD HEAVYWEIGHT CHAMPION JACK DEMPSEY defeated French prizefighter Georges Carpentier in a fourth-round knockout in Jersey City for professional boxing's first $1 million gate. Two years later at the Polo Grounds, the legendary baseball stadium of the Giants and Yankees, Dempsey knocked down Luis Angel Firpo nine times in two rounds to retain his title. After retirement, Dempsey and his wife ran a Midtown Manhattan bar that featured an eighteen-foot painting by James Montgomery Flagg of the boxer clobbering Jess Willard. The painting now hangs in the Smithsonian Institution in Washington, D.C. Mayor Ed Koch officially designated Forty-ninth and Broadway Jack Dempsey Corner in 1984. This recipe—which appears in the *Savoy Cocktail Book*, published in London in 1930—will deliver a punch like Dempsey if you go too many rounds with it.

cocktail glass

1 ounce gin
1 ounce Calvados
2 dashes absinthe
2 dashes grenadine

SHAKE ALL INGREDIENTS OVER ICE; STRAIN INTO A CHILLED COCKTAIL GLASS.

Note: You can substitute another apple-y brandy, such as Applejack,
for the Calvados and Verte de Fougerolles for the absinthe.

Dolores

THE FOLLIES CAPTURED NEW YORK'S HEART AND DOROTHY PARKER'S, TOO. AS A critic, she adored the show for its catchy songs, campy humor, and fantastic costumes. She also admired the beautiful showgirls. Writing for *Vanity Fair* in 1918, she said, "I was delighted, too, to hand it to the chorus, who fully live up to the advertisements of 'a chorus of forty under twenty,'—in most of the season's musical shows, it has been just vice versa." Former typist Kathleen Mary Rose, a statuesque British model, ranked among the first and most famous hired by Florenz Ziegfeld. He gave her the stage name Dolores, and she became a star as a stage "mannequin" who didn't sing, dance, or talk. Acclaimed as "the loveliest showgirl in the world," Dolores never cracked a smile onstage. In *Follies* spectacles such as "The Episode of Chiffon," she stood onstage as the Empress of Fashion. Dolores appeared in Ziegfeld productions from 1917 to 1921, including the *Midnight Frolic of 1919* in which she wore a white peacock costume with a ten-foot train. Afterward, she quit the stage, moved to Paris, and married a millionaire in 1923. This drink, when properly made, tastes like candy.

old-fashioned
glass

1½ ounces **Spanish brandy**
1½ ounces **cherry brandy**
1½ ounces **crème de cacao**

STIR ALL INGREDIENTS OVER ICE; SERVE ON THE ROCKS.

g costumes were fashioned for Dolores as a *Follies* star. Decades after she left Forty-second Street, fans embered her beauty. ◆ ◆ ◆

Dubonnet Cocktail

THE ALGONQUIN ROUND TABLE COLLECTIVELY ZEROED IN ON GREAT NECK, LONG Island, in the early 1920s. Its members visited the homes of fellow writer Ring Lardner and the powerful executive editor of the *New York World*, Herbert Bayard Swope. At Swope's incredible dinner parties, croquet matches and all-night dancing took place. Scott and Zelda Fitzgerald rented nearby, and Swope's parties became the inspiration for the Gatsby soirées. At a dinner one night with Governor Albert Ritchie of Maryland, the guests were quizzing the politician on the state of the union. Suddenly, a man deep in his cups burped loudly. A brief embarrassed hush ensued—until Dorothy Parker, a frequent Swope guest, deftly broke it: "I'll get the governor to pardon you," she said sweetly. The Dubonnet Cocktail, a popular Prohibition drink that originated in France, certainly appeared on the Swope table and is excellent today as an aperitif.

cocktail glass

1½ ounces dry gin
1½ ounces Dubonnet
Lemon peel

SHAKE ALL INGREDIENTS OVER CRACKED ICE, STRAIN INTO A CHILLED
COCKTAIL GLASS, AND ADD A TWIST OF LEMON PEEL.

Note: There is no substitute for Dubonnet in this cocktail.

El Presidente

One of the best vacations in the speakeasy era of 1920 to 1933 was sailing to Cuba. On that island, home to the Bacardi factory and countless bars and nightclubs, many Americans discovered cocktails made with rum for the first time. These recipes soon made their way back to the States. Among the most popular was the El Presidente, created at Bar La Florida in Havana for a now mostly forgotten president of Cuba, General Carmen Menocal.

cocktail glass

1 ounce Bacardi light rum
1 ounce dry vermouth
1 teaspoon grenadine
1 teaspoon Curaçao
Orange peel
Maraschino cherry

FILL A TALL MIXING GLASS WITH CRACKED ICE; ADD RUM AND VERMOUTH. POUR IN THE GRENADINE AND CURAÇAO, STIR, AND STRAIN INTO A CHILLED COCKTAIL GLASS. CAREFULLY TWIST THE ORANGE PEEL OVER THE SIDE OF THE GLASS; ITS ORANGEY OIL SHOULD FLOAT ON THE SURFACE OF THE DRINK. DROP IN THE ORANGE PEEL AND A MARASCHINO CHERRY.

Emperor Norton's Second Mistress

Elixir, San Francisco

EIGHT YEARS AFTER CALIFORNIA WAS GRANTED STATEHOOD, A BAR OPENED ON THE corner of Sixteenth and Guerrero in San Francisco's Mission District. More than 150 years later, Elixir continues its proud history of crafting cocktails. Proprietor H. Joseph Ehrmann, president of the Barbary Coast Conservancy of the American Cocktail, helps run San Francisco Cocktail Week and wanted to create a drink to honor a famous local figure. "Emperor Norton was a classic San Francisco icon from the Victorian era, declaring himself 'Emperor of these United States and Protector of Mexico.' He walked San Francisco between 1849 and his death in 1880, distributing his own currency (accepted by many) and invited foreign royalty to visit him. If he came into the saloon and I was behind the stick, I'd have served him."

old-fashioned
glass

4 medium California strawberries
1½ ounces Cyrus Noble bourbon
¾ ounce Tuaca

IN A MIXING CUP, MUDDLE 3 STRAWBERRIES TO JUICE. ADD BOURBON AND TUACA AND FILL WITH ICE. SHAKE HARD TO DILUTE AND THEN HAWTHORNE STRAIN INTO A LARGE OLD-FASHIONED GLASS FILLED WITH FRESH ICE. SLICE 1 STRAWBERRY HALFWAY AND PLACE ON RIM TO GARNISH.

f Emperor Norton's prophecies was a bridge linking San Francisco and Oakland. Locals still
nber him fondly. ◆ ◆ ◆

Espionage

THE FBI FILE ON DOROTHY PARKER RUNS THREE INCHES THICK. NEARLY HALF A century after her death, many portions remain redacted. The only city where Mrs. Parker ever got in trouble was Boston (see the Ward 8 recipe, page 118), so she'd be happy to know about the Espionage, dreamed up in the Kenmore Square neighborhood. "A guest was looking for a Manhattan-style cocktail, but with vodka," says manager Kevin Martin. "Since Fair Quinoa vodka carries the weight of a whiskey, it was the choice base spirit. Mixed with the floral chartreuse, multiple bitters, and two garnishes, the cocktail was born. Named for its deceiving flavor, this vodka cocktail drinks like a whiskey cocktail." Eastern Standard Kitchen & Drinks is a neighborhood brasserie with charm, knowledgeable bartenders, a wide mix of regulars—and is home to the Espionage.

lowball glass

1½ ounces Fair Quinoa vodka
¾ ounce yellow chartreuse
½ ounce Cynar liqueur
½ ounce Amaro Montenegro Italian liqueur
Lemon twist
Orange twist

MOUNT LIQUID INGREDIENTS INTO A MIXING GLASS FILLED WITH CRACKED ICE, STIR UNTIL PROPERLY DILUTED, STRAIN INTO A CHILLED LOWBALL GLASS, AND GARNISH WITH IN-AND-OUT LEMON AND ORANGE TWISTS.

Florodora

FLORODORA, A MUSICAL SHOW OF SIX BEAUTIFUL SHOWGIRLS, ENTERTAINED TURN-OF-the-century audiences. Always a sextet averaging five feet, six inches tall, the *Florodora* girls were huge celebrities when Theodore Roosevelt was president. Traveling shows played towns from coast to coast, and the cast was treated like royalty. The young women became major stars, and their exploits filled gossip columns. In 1920 the show was revived on Broadway at the Century Theatre, and Dorothy Parker panned it in *Ainslee's,* writing, "There has been an amazingly well-preserved glamour about *Florodora*. Perhaps it was a reflection of the radiance shed by those original six, the girls who 'put the sex in sextet,' as you might say." When the revival came out, so did a tasty gin cocktail that became all the rage in speakeasies.

highball glass

1½ ounces gin
½ ounce fresh lime juice
¾ ounce Framboise (raspberry liqueur)
Splash ginger ale
Lime wedge

IN A HIGHBALL GLASS FILLED WITH ICE, BUILD THE GIN, LIME JUICE, AND RASPBERRY LIQUEUR. TOP WITH GINGER ALE AND GARNISH WITH A LIME WEDGE.

Note: Framboise, the French word for "raspberry," can also be used to refer to any alcohol distilled from fruit. Because of the fruit, this cocktail has the aroma of raspberries. While Framboise usually is served in a Champagne flute, rhe Florodora breaks the tradition.

French "75"

ONLY A FEW DAYS AFTER THE 1917 WEDDING OF DOROTHY ROTHSCHILD AND EDWIN
Pond Parker II, war separated the newlyweds. Eddie went to New Jersey for
army training and then shipped out to France as a driver in the 33rd Ambulance
Corps. Dottie didn't get him back until 1919. During the Great War, a number
of future members of the Algonquin Round Table served in uniform, including
Franklin P. Adams, Herman Mankiewicz, Harold Ross, Robert E. Sherwood,
Laurence Stallings, and Alexander Woollcott. Vicious Circle civilians in Paris
included Heywood Broun, Jane Grant, Ruth Hale, and Neysa McMein.
Doughboys brought back the popular French "75," named for the 75mm
M1897, a French field gun. Irvin S. Cobb went to the front as a correspondent
for the *Saturday Evening Post* and two decades later recalled his experience of
a French "75" – "I had my first of these in a dugout in the Argonne. I couldn't tell
whether a shell or the drink hit me."

champagne flute

1 ounce gin
Juice of 1 lemon
1 teaspoon powdered sugar
Champagne

POUR THE GIN INTO THE CHAMPAGNE FLUTE. ADD THE LEMON JUICE AND SUGAR.
FILL THE REMAINDER OF THE GLASS WITH CHILLED CHAMPAGNE.

French army officers share a drink in the field, circa 1915. ◆ ◆ ◆

Gene Tunney

Beginning in 1922, Harold Ross, Jane Grant, and Alexander Woollcott lived together at 412 West Forty-seventh Street, a Hell's Kitchen duplex. Dorothy Parker and the Algonquin Round Table were frequent guests, along with top writers, cartoonists, actors, musicians, and other cultural figures. Gene Tunney was world heavyweight champion from 1926 to 1928. His two victories over Jack Dempsey remain among the most famous bouts in boxing history. The drink named for him—practically a Martini, with a little juice added—proved popular on both sides of the Atlantic.

In *Ross, The New Yorker, and Me,* Grant's account of the era, she relates the following story. One night, two drunks, thinking the house a speakeasy, tried to push their way in. Grant's friend tried to block their way.

"The kids told us it was a speakeasy," the men told her friend.

"Well, it isn't," he said, "and you'd better get out."

"Who's going to put us out? You can't," one of the drunks replied as he tried to push the friend aside.

"Well, maybe I can't, but Gene Tunney can. Hey, Gene," the friend called out.

"Aw, quit kidding," the bigger of the intruders said. Just as he was about to barge in, the heavyweight champ walked toward them, and they scattered.

cocktail glass

2 ounces gin
1 ounce French vermouth
Dash of orange juice
Dash of lemon juice
Lemon peel

SHAKE LIQUID INGREDIENTS WELL OVER CRACKED ICE. STRAIN INTO A CHILLED
COCKTAIL GLASS AND GARNISH WITH A TWIST OF LEMON PEEL.

Gene Tunney was born in New York City's Greenwich Village. He beat Jack Dempsey for the world heavyweight championship in 1926 in front of 120,500 screaming fans in Philadelphia. ◆ ◆ ◆

The pop culture icon of 1900, the Gibson Girl came from the pen of
Charles Dana Gibson. ◆ ◆ ◆

Gibson

For many years cocktail historians have debated where the Gibson originated. It could be a cousin to a pre-Prohibition drink, the "onion cocktail." The (mostly) accepted story holds that the Gibson is named for magazine illustrator Charles Dana Gibson and was created at Gramercy Park's Players Club, a society founded in 1888 for men in theater, music, and literature. In the 1880s, Gibson joined the staff of the old *Life* (not to be confused with the Henry Luce publication), a monthly humor magazine. In the 1920s, *Life* employed Robert Benchley, Dorothy Parker, Robert E. Sherwood, and many other Algonquin Round Table members. Gibson earned his renown for drawing alluring women in illustrations of high-society scenes. In 1890 he created a haughty beauty with upswept raven hair that became a symbol of the Gay Nineties: the Gibson Girl. His renditions of stylish, athletic, and alluring girls made Gibson rich. *Life* proved wildly popular through World War I, and it was Mrs. Parker's bread and butter. *The New Yorker*, debuting in 1925, was modeled partially on *Life*. Although the Gibson bears a striking resemblance to a Martini, it should not be considered just a Martini with an onion in it—and no onions, please. This is the classic World War I version.

cocktail glass

1½ ounces gin
1½ ounces dry vermouth
Maraschino cherry

IN A MIXING GLASS FILLED WITH CRACKED ICE, ADD THE LIQUID INGREDIENTS.
STIR SLOWLY AND STRAIN INTO A CHILLED COCKTAIL GLASS. GARNISH WITH A CHERRY.

Gimlet

DOROTHY PARKER AND ALEXANDER WOOLLCOTT SHARED AN ABIDING AFFECTION FOR mysteries, murder, and crime stories. One of the best practitioners of the genre, Raymond Chandler has his detective Philip Marlowe drink Gimlets in *The Long Goodbye*. Chandler said, "Alcohol is like love. The first kiss is magic, the second is intimate, the third is routine. After that you take the girl's clothes off." A proper Gimlet always includes Rose's Lime Juice, first patented in 1867. The Gimlet became a standard speakeasy drink because it was simple and fast to make, and the lime juice easily covered imperfections in what might be a bad batch of gin. Legend holds that the drink originated in the Royal Navy when ship's doctor T. O. Gimlette prescribed the drink as a medicinal tonic. Apparently Dr. Gimlette thought he was fighting scurvy by adding lime juice to the sailors' gin rations. According to the British, the only good Gimlet is a cold one, thoroughly mixed with cracked ice before serving.

cocktail glass

2 ounces gin
1 ounce Rose's lime juice
Slice of fresh lime (optional)

SHAKE LIQUID INGREDIENTS OVER ICE; STRAIN INTO A COCKTAIL GLASS. ADD OPTIONAL SLICE OF LIME.

Note: You can serve the drink neat or over ice. In the 1920s soda water was often added. If you substitute fresh lime juice for the Rose's Lime Juice, add 1 teaspoon confectioner's sugar. For effect, frost the rim of the glass by dipping it into lime juice, then granulated sugar. Chill the sugar-frosted glass in the refrigerator before preparing the drink.

Gin Fizz

THE FIRST TIME DOROTHY PARKER SAW PARIS, SHE WAS THIRTY-TWO AND BROKE. SHE sailed from New York in early 1926 with Robert Benchley and Ernest Hemingway aboard the *President Roosevelt*. Her visit to the French Riviera provided Mrs. Parker with a wealth of material for many years. In 1929 *The New Yorker* published a short piece by her set on the Mediterranean, a boozy conversation between a couple of Gin Fizz-guzzling Americans, a ridiculous playboy and a silly socialite. In "The Cradle of Civilization" the young man orders another round of drinks in his bad French. "Oh, garçon. Encore deux jeen feezes, tout de suite," he said. "And mettez un peu more de jeen in them cette fois, baby." Fizzes are sour-based cocktails with mandatory additions of club soda and lemon juice. A Gin Fizz is served in a highball glass of 8 to 12 ounces, topped with club soda.

highball glass

2 ounces gin
¾ ounce fresh lemon juice
1 teaspoon superfine sugar or simple syrup
Club soda
Mint sprig

SHAKE THE GIN, LEMON JUICE, AND SUGAR OVER CRACKED ICE AND STRAIN INTO A 10-OUNCE HIGHBALL GLASS FILLED WITH ICE. FILL THE REMAINDER OF THE GLASS WITH COLD CLUB SODA. GARNISH WITH MINT.

Note: There are dozens of variations of the Gin Fizz. Add a whole egg for a Royal Fizz, or add ¾ ounce orange juice and 1 teaspoon simple syrup to make a Texas Fizz. A teaspoon of cream in the drink makes it a Cream Fizz.

Gin Rickey

IN *THE GREAT GATSBY*, TOM BUCHANAN SERVES FOUR GIN RICKEYS ON A BLAZING hot afternoon on Long Island. The cocktail is perfect on a summer day, and in the book Jay Gatsby serves the drink often at his Gold Coast estate, employing a cadre of bartenders to mix them for his gala parties. As F. Scott Fitzgerald writes, "Every Friday five crates of oranges and lemons arrived from a fruiterer in New York—every Monday these same oranges and lemons left his back door in a pyramid of pulpless halves." The Gin Rickey was one of the most popular drinks of the era. Its creation traces back to Joe Rickey, a Capitol Hill lobbyist, to whom the drink was served at Shoemaker's, located on Pennsylvania Avenue, in the 1890s.

collins glass

1½ ounces gin
½ ounce fresh lime juice
Club soda
Lime wedge

POUR GIN AND LIME JUICE INTO A COLLINS GLASS FILLED WITH ICE CUBES.
FILL WITH COLD CLUB SODA AND STIR. ADD THE WEDGE OF LIME AND SERVE.

Note: This drink has countless variations; for any substituted potable, the drink
is then called by the liquor used, such as a Rum Rickey and so on.

Dorothy Parker in Hollywood

♦ ♦ ♦

Dorothy Parker's first trip to Los Angeles came in late 1928, when she signed a three-month contract with MGM for $300 a week. A gossip columnist reported that December on Mrs. Parker's transition to screenwriter:

No movie contract could keep her at work by merely cloistering her in a remote office at the far end of the longest corridor in a dismal Culver City office building. She has managed to turn this cell into quite a salon by a device that many lonelyhearts might find helpful. When the sign painter arrived to put her name on the door, she bribed him to leave it off and substitute instead the simple legend: GENTLEMEN.

When her contract ended and with no screen credits to her name, Mrs. Parker returned to New York City.

She stayed away from the West Coast for five years. In 1934, following her marriage to actor-writer Alan Campbell, the couple moved to California on a temporary basis. They arrived in a state of semi-destitution in an open-topped Ford with two dogs. Within a week, they were signed to a studio for $5,000 a week and living in a friend's huge home in Beverly Hills. The couple lived in rented mansions in Beverly Hills, stayed in the Château Marmont and Garden of Allah on Sunset Boulevard, and, when funds ran low, they moved into a not-so-great West Hollywood bungalow at 8983 Norma Place.

As a writing team, they worked on more than thirty pictures. In *Hanging On in Paradise*, author Fred Lawrence Guiles described their partnership, with Campbell playing a key role:

It was he who sat at the typewriter and did the real work of putting down on paper the technical and special language of the scriptwriter. Dorothy would sit nearby, often knitting, as Alan might ask, 'Shall we make the mother a washerwoman,' and Dorothy might say, 'Oh yes, by all means, a washerwoman.' Then she would read over what Alan had written and edit it and write in some witty dialogue, elevating the competent to the penetrating and, sometimes, the splendid.

Dorothy and Alan earned their only Academy Award nomination as a team for the original screenplay to *A Star Is Born,* since remade twice. They were nominated for best screenplay in 1937, along with Robert Carson, but the Oscar went to *The Life of Emile Zola.*

In 1935 Dorothy Parker and Alan Campbell were signed to Paramount Pictures as a screenwriting team. ◆ ◆ ◆

The couple worked steadily into the 1930s, but the experience proved rocky. Stories of Mrs. Parker's conflicts with the studios are legendary. After being scolded by Samuel Goldwyn, who told her, "You haven't got a great audience, and you know why? Because you don't give people what they want," Mrs. Parker softly replied: "But Mr. Goldwyn,

---

Dottie on DVD: Five Films She Co-Wrote
Hands Across the Table (1935)
Suzy (1936)
A Star Is Born (1937)
The Cowboy and the Lady (1938)
Smash-Up: The Story of a Woman (1947)

---

people don't *know* what they want until you *give* it to them." Goldwyn exploded, saying, "Wisecracks. I told you there's no money in wisecracks. People want a happy ending." To which she responded: "I know this will come as a shock to you, Mr. Goldwyn, but in all history, which has held billions and billions of human beings, not a single one ever had a happy ending."

After Campbell joined the army, Mrs. Parker lived in Hollywood and New York, working on short stories and screenplays. After a period of separation, divorce, and remarriage, the couple worked on a handful of scripts in the 1950s. After her husband's death, Mrs. Parker returned to New York, at the age of seventy.

"You just don't know how I love it — how I get up every morning and want to kiss the pavement . . . Hollywood smells like a laundry," she told Ward Morehouse of the *New York World-Telegram and Sun.* "The beautiful vegetables taste as if they were raised in trunks, and at those wonderful supermarkets you find that the vegetables are all wax. The flowers out there smell like dirty, old dollar bills."

In 1941 her friend Budd Schulberg wrote *What Makes Sammy Run?* about screenwriting. Mrs. Parker said, "I never thought anyone could put Hollywood — the true shittiness of it — between covers."

55

The Happy Herbie

The Edison, Los Angeles

WALT DISNEY HIMSELF TAPPED TWO ALGONQUIN ROUND TABLE MEMBERS TO APPEAR in animated feature films. Deems Taylor narrates the classic *Fantasia* (1940), and Robert Benchley plays himself in *The Reluctant Dragon* (1941). Disney artist and "imagineer" Herbert Ryman art-directed *Fantasia* and *Dumbo,* and in the 1950s Disney tapped Ryman to draw the concept art for Disneyland, which became the blueprint for the amusement park. Inside a hundred-year-old former power plant in Downtown Los Angeles lies The Edison, a lounge that evokes the city's romantic past. John Maraffi, director of spirits, created the Happy Herbie for a fundraiser for the Ryman Foundation (Ryman.org), which provides fine art training to teenagers. "Although it's a twenty-first-century cocktail, the flavor and color evoke the style of a classic cocktail," says Barbara Jacobs, who runs The Edison. "It sends the guest to Disneyland, with apples and oranges rounding out the vision of the Happiest Place on Earth."

cocktail glass

2 ounces Templeton rye whiskey
½ ounce GreenBar jasmine liqueur
½ ounce freshly squeezed lemon juice
½ ounce simple syrup
3 dashes Bar Keep apple bitters
Orange peel

SHAKE ALL LIQUID INGREDIENTS OVER ICE; STRAIN INTO A CHILLED
COCKTAIL GLASS. GARNISH WITH ORANGE PEEL.

Hemingway Daiquiri

Bar La Florida Style

DOROTHY PARKER NEVER MADE IT TO CUBA, BUT HER FRENEMY, ERNEST HEMINGWAY, famously did. The two writers did sail to France aboard the same cruise ship in early 1926, however. One story of that journey holds that Hemingway had forgotten his portable typewriter, so Mrs. Parker loaned him her Underwood. For whatever reason, he pitched it over the side of the ship. After Hemingway began his love affair with Cuba, he named Bar La Florida—located on Obispo and Montserrate Streets and still in operation—his favorite Havana watering hole. Hemingway welcomed friends such as Gary Cooper and Spencer Tracy there, and in 2003 a life-size statue of the writer was installed in his favorite spot. Bar La Florida, in existence since 1819, claims to have invented the Daiquiri. Hemingway preferred his served as a double, over a single serving of ice, or frozen. This recipe comes from the bar's own 1935 menu.

highball glass

2 ounces Bacardi white rum
½ ounce fresh lime juice
1 teaspoon grapefruit juice
1 teaspoon maraschino liqueur

FILL A BLENDER WITH 2 CUPS CRUSHED ICE, ADD ALL THE INGREDIENTS, AND BLEND. POUR INTO A CHILLED HIGHBALL GLASS.

Note: Using a blender makes the daiquiri frozen or frappe.

Highball

THE NAME FOR THIS DRINK COMES FROM THE NINETEENTH-CENTURY RAILROAD DAYS, when raising a signal—a ball on a long pole—meant engines could proceed at full steam. When New York bartender Patrick Duffy invented the drink in the 1890s, it was taken to mean how fast the drink could be assembled. All highballs are meant to be simple to mix, to be served over ice, and to refresh. In a tall glass it's a Highball; in an old-fashioned glass, it's a Lowball.

highball glass

2 ounces Scotch, bourbon, or rye
Club soda or ginger ale
Lemon twist (optional)

THE KEY TO A GOOD HIGHBALL IS BUILDING IT. START WITH THE ALCOHOL. FIRST, POUR THE WHISKEY INTO A CHILLED GLASS FILLED WITH ICE CUBES. TOP WITH COLD CLUB SODA OR GINGER ALE, STIRRING GENTLY. IF DESIRED, DROP IN A LEMON TWIST.

◆ ◆ ◆

This is a nice highball, isn't it? Well, well, well, to think of me having real Scotch; I'm out of the bush leagues at last. It will be nice to see the effect of veritable whisky upon one who has been accustomed only to the simpler forms of entertainment.

—from Dorothy Parker's classic 1928 short story, "Just a Little One," about a night in a speakeasy, published in *The New Yorker*

Horse's Neck

JUST ONE SPEAKEASY PROPRIETOR earned the sobriquet "Queen of the Nightclubs," and that was Texas Guinan. A larger-than-life bottle blonde with a big smile and bigger personality, Texas was beloved by boozehounds and newspaper gossip columnists. The authorities were constantly hauling her off to jail, which only added to her reputation. She wore a necklace made of handcuff keys, and during raids she asked her band to perform "The Prisoner's Song" as she was led out. Because Texas supplied the ginger ale if her customers brought

Texas Guinan was a larger-than-life speakeasy owner and performer. ◆ ◆ ◆

the booze, here's a famous Jazz Age cocktail that depends on it. This recipe comes from Rob Chirico's *Field Guide to Cocktails*.

highball glass

Orange peel
2 ounces bourbon
4 ounces ginger ale

CAREFULLY CARVE A LONG PIECE OF PEEL, 1½ INCHES WIDE, FROM THE ORANGE, THEN WRAP THE SPIRAL AROUND SEVERAL ICE CUBES IN A HIGHBALL GLASS. SOME OF THE EXCESS PEEL SHOULD HANG OVER THE SIDE OF THE GLASS, LIKE A HORSE'S NECK. ADD THE BOURBON AND COLD GINGER ALE AND STIR.

Jack Rose

IN *THE SUN ALSO RISES*, JAKE BARNES HAS A JACK ROSE WHILE WAITING IN VAIN FOR the "damned good-looking" Lady Brett Ashley in a Paris hotel bar. Ernest Hemingway added the reference when the drink was popular in the 1920s. Hemingway was in Paris with the Spanish surrealist filmmaker Luis Buñuel. "If you were to ask me if I'd ever had the bad luck to miss my daily cocktail," Buñuel said, "I'd have to say that I doubt it; where certain things are concerned, I plan ahead."

cocktail glass

2 ounces applejack or Calvados
½ ounce fresh lime or lemon juice
2–4 dashes grenadine

SHAKE ALL INGREDIENTS OVER ICE; STRAIN INTO A CHILLED COCKTAIL GLASS.

Note: Applejack is the American term for 80 to 100 proof apple brandy aged two years in wooden casks. Calvados comes from France and is also a popular apple brandy.

Jean Harlow

THE CONNECTION BETWEEN THE ORIGINAL BLONDE BOMBSHELL AND DOROTHY Parker is a strong one. Mrs. Parker and her husband, Alan Campbell, wrote one of Jean Harlow's best films, the 1936 MGM comedy *Suzy*. One of the pivotal scenes depicts Harlow and Cary Grant, playing a cabaret singer and a pilot, trading wisecracks in a French bistro over little glasses of Cointreau. This namesake drink offers a variation on the Martini, and this recipe allegedly was Harlow's favorite cocktail.

cocktail glass

2 ounces white rum
2 ounces sweet vermouth
Lemon peel

POUR THE RUM AND VERMOUTH INTO A SHAKER FILLED WITH CRACKED ICE.
DEPENDING ON YOUR PREFERENCE, YOU CAN EITHER SHAKE OR SLOWLY STIR IT.
POUR INTO A CHILLED COCKTAIL GLASS AND GARNISH WITH THE LEMON PEEL.

Jean Harlow, Cary Grant, and George Davis in *Suzy*. ◆ ◆ ◆

Josephine Baker

FREDA JOSEPHINE MCDONALD WAS BORN POOR IN ST. LOUIS, MISSOURI, IN 1906, but by the time of her death in 1975, the dancer had attained global recognition as one of the most sought-after black entertainers. McDonald changed her name to Josephine Baker when she was nineteen and moved to Paris, where her audience was almost exclusively white. Historian Ann Douglas says in *Terrible Honesty* that Baker

> *liked to turn up in a Poiret gown, but this was never her primary look. Onstage and off, she was noted for something close to nudity, nudity accentuated by a belt of bananas around her hips or a long feather curling provocatively between her legs, and at the most unexpected moments she would start mugging: she'd cross her eyes, throw her bronze limbs akimbo in a comical kaleidoscope of fractured motion, turning on the glamorous and provocative image she'd created but a moment before.*

This recipe comes from the 1935 menu of Havana's most popular bar-restaurant, La Florida.

cocktail glass

1½ ounces Cognac
1½ ounces port wine
¾ ounce apricot brandy
1 teaspoon sugar
1 egg yolk
Cinnamon
Lemon peel

SHAKE ALL THE LIQUID INGREDIENTS AND SUGAR WELL OVER ICE. STRAIN INTO
A LARGE COCKTAIL GLASS FILLED WITH CRACKED ICE. SPREAD A PINCH OF
CINNAMON ON TOP OF THE DRINK AND GARNISH WITH A LEMON TWIST.

Note: The original recipe calls for Soberano Cognac, a Spanish brand not easily available in America. You can substitute Hennessey V.S. ("very special").

The Knickerbocker Cocktail

WASHINGTON IRVING, NEW YORK'S FIRST professional author, wrote his classic *History of New York* in 1809, penned by the pseudonymous "Diedrich Knickerbocker." Over time the name came to signify natives of the city or state of New York. On the southeast corner of Forty-second Street and Broadway, millionaire real estate scion John Jacob Astor IV built the lavish fifteen-story luxury Hotel Knickerbocker, which opened in 1906. Broadway regulars loved its swanky bar and restaurant. Astor commissioned Maxfield Parrish to paint a mural for the bar, and the thirty-foot-wide *Old King Cole* now hangs over the bar in the St. Regis, another Astor hotel. The Algonquin Round Table often attended

The grand old Knickerbocker still stands in Times Square, but, no longer a hotel, today it's an office building and a storefront for selling T-shirts. ◆ ◆ ◆

midnight parties in the Knickerbocker, which was often home to theater stars such as George M. Cohan. The red brick beaux arts building, with its eye-catching copper mansard roof, is the only grand hotel left in Times Square. It was gutted long ago for office and retail space, a victim of the Great Depression, but the Knickerbocker Cocktail carries on the bar's name.

cocktail glass

2 ounces rum
1 teaspoon raspberry syrup
1 teaspoon fresh lemon juice
2 dashes Curaçao
1 chunk pineapple

STIR LIQUID INGREDIENTS WITH ICE. STRAIN INTO A CHILLED
COCKTAIL GLASS. DROP IN THE PINEAPPLE CHUNK.

The Last Word

THE YEAR 1916 SAW THE FOUNDING OF THE *DETROIT ATHLETIC CLUB NEWS* FOR THE 10,000 members of the private club in Michigan. During the Jazz Age, the *DAC News* bought freelance pieces from some of the top humorists in the country: Robert Benchley, Ring Lardner, Groucho Marx, Dorothy Parker, Frank Sullivan, and James Thurber. The DAC, which is still going strong, has a fabulous bar where the Last Word was created by vaudeville star Frank J. Fogarty, a native of Red Hook, Brooklyn. In 1912, Fogarty, a comedian and performer for twenty-five years, had won the *New York Morning Telegraph* contest for most popular performer in vaudeville. After retiring, he went to work for the Brooklyn borough president. On his deathbed in 1925, Fogarty's last words were a request to hear "Fanny Dear" on the radio. He lost consciousness before WEAF could broadcast the song, but the song was played at his funeral. This recipe comes from *Zelda* magazine.

cocktail glass

1 ounce gin
1 ounce maraschino liqueur
1 ounce green chartreuse
1 ounce fresh lime juice

SHAKE ALL INGREDIENTS OVER ICE; STRAIN INTO A CHILLED COCKTAIL GLASS.

Loud Speaker

WHEN RADIO BROADCASTING BECAME POPULAR, PRODUCERS TAPPED THE TALENTS OF the Vicious Circle. Among the early radio stars was Franklin P. Adams—"I don't understand the principle of the radio, nor for that matter the telephone or the telegraph. Don't explain it to me; I don't get it."—who served as a weekly panelist on the hit quiz show *Information Please*. CBS hired Deems Taylor to present classical music programming, and Alexander Woollcott, in a smooth transition in the 1930s from newspapers to radio, also broadcast coast to coast. Round Table writers found their material easily adapted to radio scripts: Robert Benchley, Edna Ferber, and Dorothy Parker all cashed nice checks from radio networks for broadcasting their short stories. Naturally a cocktail was dreamed up to celebrate the new medium. The Loud Speaker appeared in the 1930 *Savoy Cocktail Book* in London.

cocktail glass

¾ ounce dry gin
¾ ounce brandy
¼ ounce Cointreau
¼ ounce lemon juice

SHAKE ALL INGREDIENTS OVER ICE; STRAIN INTO A CHILLED COCKTAIL GLASS.

◆ ◆ ◆

Along with this recipe came the following admonishment: "This it is that gives to radio announcers their peculiar enunciation. Three of them will produce oscillation, and after five it is possible to reach the osculation stage."

Love Cocktail

She made her bones by writing light verse about her broken heart, and it's on her poetry that most of Dorothy Parker's reputation stands. Just a few titles give a sense of her devotion to the subject: "Love Song," "Men I'm Not Married To," "One Perfect Rose," and "Song of a Contented Heart," the last of which tellingly predates "Song of a Hopeful Heart" by a year.

Mrs. Parker's 1933 Anacreontic poem "The Lady's Reward" ends with:

Be you wise and never sad,
You will get your lovely lad.
Never serious be, nor true,
And your wish will come to you—
And if that makes you happy, kid,
You'll be the first it ever did.

The Hotel Wallick in Times Square served this cocktail in 1917.

cocktail glass

1½ ounces sloe gin
1 egg white
1 teaspoon lemon juice
1 teaspoon raspberry syrup

SHAKE ALL INGREDIENTS OVER CRACKED ICE. STRAIN AND SERVE IN A CHILLED COCKTAIL GLASS.

Note: No substitutions allowed for this drink, because these ingredients,
when mixed properly, create a drink that comes out blood red.

You know how you ought to be with men? You should always be aloof, you should never let them know you like them, you must on no account let them feel that they are of any importance to you, you must be wrapped up in your own concerns, you may never let them lose sight of the fact that you are superior, you must be, in short, a regular stuffed chemise. And if you could see what I've been doing!

—Parker's advice to the fairer sex in 1928

Mamie Taylor

AROUND THE TIME WILLIAM MCKINLEY WAS IN THE WHITE HOUSE, A BALLERINA ASKED for a drink at a summer resort on Lake Ontario, and the legend of how the beautiful Mamie Taylor took in hand a whiskey and ginger ale pick-me-up entered the cocktail history books. Legendary publisher James Gordon Bennett ran the recipe in the *New York Herald,* considering it news. In 1921 the *New York Times* published a Prohibition lament: "If we ever build a wall in America it will most likely be along the Canadian and Mexican borders for the purpose of keeping such objectionable characters as John Barleycorn and Mamie Taylor from leaving The Land of the Spree and Home of Knave and contaminating our own glorious Hearth of the Home brewed Hootch." Highballs formed a huge part of speakeasy culture, so the Mamie Taylor proved popular. Miss Taylor isn't remembered for anything else except this cocktail, and this recipe comes from a 1936 collection of whiskey highball recipes.

highball glass

1½ ounces American blended whiskey
Juice of half a lime
Ginger ale

FILL A HIGHBALL GLASS WITH CRACKED ICE. POUR IN THE WHISKEY
AND LIME JUICE, THEN FILL WITH COLD GINGER ALE.

Manhattan Cocktail

A CLASSIC—AND COMPLETELY NEW YORK CREATION—IS THE MANHATTAN COCKTAIL. It comes from the Manhattan Club, a gentlemen's social club that opened in 1865 on Fifth Avenue and Fifteenth Street. Its most famous member was August Belmont Jr.: grandson of Commodore Perry, the sportsman who transformed horseracing into a high-stakes industry as well as financed construction of New York's first subway line. The Manhattan Cocktail came into being, the story goes, while he served as club president, and it became wildly popular during Prohibition. The drink appears in Truman Capote's famous novella *Breakfast at Tiffany's* as one of Holly Golightly's favorites, and Marilyn Monroe drinks one in *Some Like It Hot*. This recipe comes from a 1936 guide by Irvin S. Cobb, who called it "one of America's greatest contributions to civilization. If the recipe given is too dry for you, make the drink half and half, whiskey and Italian vermouth."

cocktail glass

2 ounces rye
1 ounce sweet vermouth
Dash Angostura bitters
Maraschino cherry

STIR LIQUID INGREDIENTS WITH CRACKED ICE, STRAIN, AND GARNISH WITH THE CHERRY.

Note: To make a Cuban Manhattan, substitute rum for the rye and add another ounce of vermouth.

The Marquis

Flûte, New York

"TEXAS GUINAN, IN HER FASHION, DURING THE BOOM TIMES OF THE TWENTIES COMBINED the curious and admirable traits of Queen Elizabeth, Machiavelli, Tex Rickard, P. T. Barnum, and Ma Pettingill," wrote Stanley Walker, city editor of the *New York Herald Tribune*. "She was known as Queen of the Night Clubs. Her greeting 'Hello, sucker!' became the watchword of boobtraps from Wall Street to Hollywood." One of "Queen of the Nightclubs" Texas Guinan's regular spots was Club Intime, at 205 West Fifty-fourth Street, which operates today as Flûte. Down a flight of stairs off Broadway lies an intimate lounge opened by Hervé Rousseau and run with a tradition of flowing Champagne and Prohibition parties featuring vintage drinks. Ne'er-do-well bartenders at Flûte invented a drink and named it for another Frenchman who liked a good time, the Marquis de Sade. Topped with Champagne, it makes for a grand tribute in the spot once occupied by Texas and her showgirls.

 cocktail glass

1 ounce Grand Marnier
1 ounce full-bodied red wine
1 ounce orange juice
¼ ounce lime juice
¼ ounce simple syrup
Champagne
Orange slice

SHAKE GRAND MARNIER, WINE, JUICES, AND SIMPLE SYRUP WELL OVER ICE AND POUR INTO A LARGE COCKTAIL GLASS. TOP WITH CHAMPAGNE AND GARNISH WITH THE ORANGE SLICE.

Note: You can substitute another orange-flavored brandy liqueur for the Grand Marnier.

Standing on a piano and waving a police whistle and noisemaker, Texas Guinan welcomes her customers in an illustration by Joseph Golinkin. ◆ ◆ ◆

Martini

MORE INK HAS BEEN SPILLED ABOUT THE MARTINI THAN ANY OTHER COCKTAIL. IT'S THE king of all mixed drinks, and there are entire books devoted to it. Beverage historians argue the history of the Martini with the kind of passion usually exhibited among Civil War reenactors. Into the middle of Martini lore falls the little woman from the Upper West Side—an avowed Highball fan—commonly believed to be the number one proponent of the Martini in the Jazz Age. But the fact is, Dorothy Parker never mentions imbibing a Martini in any of her poems or fiction. In none of her books does the famous gin-soaked quatrain appear:

> I love a martini—
> But two at the most.
> Three, I'm under the table;
> Four, I'm under the host.

If she did in fact generate these twenty words, the text certainly isn't under copyright. Which is good news for the Martini tchotchke industry, which regularly slaps it on glasses, coasters, and T-shirts. But that hardly matters to Martini fans, who eagerly raise their glasses to their favorite version of the gin classic. (We're talking gin only—vodka is for heathens.) The Martini, with just two ingredients, has been beloved since the late nineteenth century, depending on which of the many origin stories you want to believe. It has made countless appearances in novels such as *A Farewell to Arms* and vintage films including *The Thin Man*. In the Oscar-nominated screenplay to *Smash-Up,* which Mrs. Parker and Frank Cavett wrote, Carleton Young tells a crowd, "The rest of you can get your noses out of those martinis for a minute!" The Martini has survived changing tastes across two world wars, the Great Depression, and the wildly changing culture at the end of the last century.

"I love a martini –
but two at the most.
Three I'm under the table;
Four, I'm under the host."
Dorothy Parker

Cocktail napkin from the Blue Bar
of the Algonquin Hotel. ◆ ◆ ◆

cocktail glass

MARTINI
2 ounces gin
½ to 1 ounce dry vermouth

DRY MARTINI
2 ½ ounces gin
1 tablespoon dry vermouth

DIRTY MARTINI
2½ ounces gin
1 tablespoon dry vermouth
1 teaspoon olive brine

EXTRA-DRY MARTINI
2½ ounces gin
1 teaspoon dry vermouth

SWEET MARTINI
2½ ounces gin
1 ounce sweet gin
1 ounce sweet vermouth
1 dash orange bitters
1 dash Curaçao

FOR ANY MARTINI, SHAKE INGREDIENTS WELL OVER CRACKED ICE. THE MORE YOU
SHAKE, THE COLDER THE DRINK WILL BE. STRAIN INTO A COCKTAIL GLASS—CHILLED IF
POSSIBLE IN A FREEZER—AND ALWAYS SERVE STRAIGHT UP. GARNISH WITH A TWIST OF
LEMON PEEL OR OLIVE. THE GIN-TO-VERMOUTH RATIO DETERMINES THE DRYNESS OF
A MARTINI; THE LESS VERMOUTH, THE DRIER THE DRINK. IN THE 1930S THE MARTINI HAD
MUCH MORE VERMOUTH, AND IN THE 1940S THE GIN-TO-VERMOUTH RATIO WAS 2:1.

◆ ◆ ◆

Why don't you slip out of that wet coat and into a dry
martini? I'd offer you a whiskey sour, but that would
mean thinking up a new joke.

—Robert Benchley to Ginger Rogers in the 1942
motion picture *The Major and the Minor*

There is something about a Martini,

Ere the dining and dancing begin,

And to tell you the truth,

It is not the Vermouth—

I think that perhaps it's the gin.

—Ogden Nash, *A Drink with Something in It*

Mary Pickford

MARY PICKFORD AND DOUGLAS FAIRBANKS, A POWER COUPLE AND THE BIGGEST STARS of the silent film era, were also longtime residents of the Algonquin Hotel and close personal friends of general manager Frank Case. *Robin Hood* opened in 1922, and the couple rented a suite at the hotel when the film premiered in New York. Fairbanks brought along his bow and arrow and—to the delight of newspaper reporters and shock of his wife and Case—showed off his shooting skills on the hotel roof. Pickford, America's first sweetheart, made almost 250 films from 1908 to 1935. The drink that bears her name was a sensation from coast to coast and in Europe, but this recipe comes from Havana's Bar La Florida 1935 cocktail guide.

cocktail glass

1 ounce Bacardi rum
1 ounce pineapple juice
1 teaspoon grenadine
6 drops maraschino liqueur
Maraschino cherry

THIS DRINK MUST BE VERY COLD TO BE GOOD, SO SHAKE LIQUID INGREDIENTS WELL
OVER ENOUGH CRACKED ICE TO FILL THREE QUARTERS OF THE SHAKER. STRAIN
INTO A CHILLED COCKTAIL GLASS AND GARNISH WITH THE CHERRY. WHEN *GOURMET*
WROTE ABOUT THIS DRINK IN 1943, IT WAS ALREADY CALLED AN "OLD FAVORITE."

Mary Pickford and Douglas Fairbanks married in 1920, a year after they founded the United Artists film studio in partnership with Charlie Chaplin and D. W. Griffith. ◆ ◆ ◆

◆ ◆ ◆

"Mary Pickford has three good ears," Frank Case wrote. "She can sit at the table, hear what the man to her right is saying, follow the conversation at the left, and when you, at the extreme other end, try to sneak in a remark you don't want her to hear, she will call the entire length of the table, 'I'll see you later about that.'"

A Toast to the
Algonquin Round Table

◆ ◆ ◆

When publicists Murdock Pemberton and John Peter Toohey took *New York Times* drama critic Alexander Woollcott to lunch at the Algonquin Hotel, they just as easily could have opted for someplace else. The Astor Hotel lay closer to the *Times* offices on West Forty-third Street, and the Knickerbocker was fancier—but they picked the Algonquin . . . which, granted, stood across the street from where they worked, the now demolished Hippodrome Theater. The Algonquin also had a pastry chef on staff named Sarah Victor, and Woollcott had a sweet tooth.

The publicists wanted to get their new show into the newspaper. Woollcott had just returned from France, where he'd spent the previous eighteen months in an ill-fitting army uniform. By June 1919 most of the veterans had resumed their old jobs, and Woollcott delighted in telling war stories in the restaurant. Pemberton and Toohey struck out with getting press for their show, but they did hatch a plan. Going back to their office and with the help of another publicity genius, William B. Murray, they concocted a welcome-home luncheon for the rotund critic. They invited writers, editors, publicists, and actors. The group went to the Pergola Room (today the Oak Room) at the Algonquin and had a roaring good time. Woollcott, who always loved being the center of attention, was in his element. Jokes, stories, and laughs filled the room. As the friends left the hotel to go back to work, someone asked: Why not do this again?

For the next six or seven years, about six times a week, the Vicious Circle met at the Algonquin Hotel, managed by Frank Case, who lived on the top floor and was raising two teenagers. He discerningly saw the value of so many famous New Yorkers coming to the restaurant each day, so he moved the group to the main restaurant on the north end of the lobby. Case set up a large round table that could seat approximately sixteen. Some thirty members of the Round Table came and went over the years, and eleven of them appear in the 2002 painting by Natalie Ascencios that hangs in the hotel today.

The writers Franklin P. Adams, Robert Benchley, Heywood Broun, Marc Connelly, Edna Ferber, Jane Grant, Ruth Hale, George S. Kaufman, Margaret Leech, Herman J. Mankiewicz, Dorothy Parker, Robert E. Sherwood, Laurence Stallings, Donald Ogden Stewart, and Frank Sullivan joined editors Beatrice B. Kaufman, Harold Ross, and Arthur H. Samuels. Poet John V. A. Weaver married one of the actresses of the group, Broadway star Peggy Wood. Margalo Gillmore, who starred in early Eugene O'Neill plays, was another actress at the table. Harpo Marx joined in 1924, leaving his brothers out.

Neysa McMein, the most sought-after magazine cover artist of the era, hosted the group at her studio. Broadway producer Brock Pemberton, who later cofounded the Tony Awards, was invited by his younger brother, Murdock. John Peter Toohey was another press agent at the table, as were William B. Murray and David A. Wallace, and among the most popular members was composer and music critic Deems Taylor.

The group swiftly became the most-remembered gathering of literary figures of the twentieth century. But why do we remember them at all? Most wrote for daily newspapers, and what they said or talked about appeared very quickly, courtesy of their fellow columnists. Adams, best known by his initials, F.P.A., helmed a daily column that relied on contributions. When he ran poems and stories by the group, attention followed immediately. Wire services picked up the wisecracks and repartee from the columnists, and their words appeared in hundreds of newspapers nationwide. Herewith some of the best:

"Don't think I'm not incoherent." —*Harold Ross*

"Repartee is what you wish you'd said." —*Heywood Broun*

"Being an old maid is like death by drowning, a really delightful sensation after you cease to struggle." —*Edna Ferber*

"When I was born I owed twelve dollars." —George S. Kaufman

"My friends will tell you that Woollcott is a nasty old snipe. Don't believe them. [They] are a pack of simps who move their lips when they read." —Aleck Woollcott

"It took me 15 years to discover that I had no talent for writing, but I couldn't give it up because by that time I was too famous." —Robert Benchley

The Round Table also gave us *The New Yorker*, dreamed up at the hotel by Harold Ross and Jane Grant. The couple launched the magazine in February 1925, using their Round Table connections and listing the magazine's "editorial board" as Adams, Benchley, Mrs. Parker, and others, when no such group existed. Mrs. Parker wrote drama reviews for the debut issue and sold fiction to it until the 1950s, and most of the group contributed to it in some way.

The Vicious Circle wrote best-selling books and hit plays. Some of them worked in silent films, radio, talking pictures, and even early television. They left their collective mark on all areas of mass media in ways both large and small. Mrs. Parker takes credit for coining "What the hell?" while Kaufman and Connelly, needing an imaginary product in their play, dreamed up the "widget."

The Algonquin remains the most renowned literary hotel in New York City for good reason. At the Plaza lived a children's book character; the Chelsea rented rooms to writers of all stripes. But the Algonquin offered a place for collaboration, admiration, and networking that persists today. Walk into the lobby, and you won't know who they are, but editors and writers are sitting in those chairs.

Matilda

Algonquin Hotel, New York

THE TRADITION OF A LOBBY CAT AT THE ALGONQUIN HOTEL BEGAN IN 1930, ACCORDING to hotel lore. At the time, Frank Case owned the hotel, and legendary actor John Barrymore was a longtime and favorite resident. Barrymore's sister, Ethel, kept a suite in the hotel, and their uncle, actor John Drew, lived in the hotel for nearly twenty years. According to the story passed down by the staff, one day Case adopted a stray. Barrymore told Case that since the Algonquin had a literary and theatrical clientele, he couldn't give the feline a common name, so Case called him Hamlet, after Barrymore's most famous stage role. Since then, all male cats that live at the hotel have been named Hamlet; years later a female was acquired and christened Matilda (nobody knows why). Since the 1990s a succession of Matildas has ruled the Algonquin. The hotel has promoted the cat to executive status; she has her own e-mail account, Twitter account, and gets fan mail. You can usually spot Matilda on the front desk, behind the warm desktop computer, or on a luggage cart. Every August the hotel throws a birthday party for the cat, raising money for animal adoptions in front of the building. The breed, ragdoll, means she is quite content to be petted. The Matilda cocktail has been a favorite in the Blue Bar for many years.

cocktail glass

2 ounces vodka
2 ounces Cointreau
1 ounce orange juice
1 ounce lime juice
Champagne
Orange slice

SHAKE VODKA, COINTREAU, AND JUICES WELL OVER ICE; POUR INTO A COCKTAIL GLASS. TOP WITH CHAMPAGNE AND GARNISH WITH THE ORANGE SLICE.

Metropolitan

THE LONG-VANISHED METROPOLITAN HOTEL OPENED AT THE CORNER OF BROADWAY AND Prince Street in 1853 in what is today Manhattan's SoHo neighborhood. The six-story building in the Italian palazzo style, the city's second luxury hotel, boasted hot and cold running water in its 500 rooms. In its ballroom entertainer P. T. Barnum hosted the 1863 wedding reception for General Tom Thumb and Lavinia Warren, who stood two feet, eight inches tall. *The Modern Bartender's Guide*, written by O. H. Byron and published in 1884, included a brandy and vermouth Metropolitan cocktail. It is sometimes attributed to the city's most famous bartender, "Professor" Jerry Thomas, hired by the hotel after the Civil War. The Metropolitan was demolished in 1895, but its namesake cocktail lives on.

old-fashioned
glass

1½ ounces brandy
1½ ounces sweet vermouth
½ teaspoon simple syrup
1–2 dashes Angostura bitters
Maraschino cherry

SHAKE LIQUID INGREDIENTS OVER CRACKED ICE; STRAIN INTO AN OLD-FASHIONED GLASS
FILLED WITH ICE CUBES. GARNISH WITH THE CHERRY.

Note: Don't confuse this drink with any modern recipes that share its
name, including the 1990s variation on a Cosmopolitan.

$\bigcirc$illionaire

DID ANYONE WRITE MORE ABOUT MONEY THAN DOROTHY PARKER? "I HATE ALMOST all rich people but I think I'd be darling at it," she allegedly uttered. "If you want to know what God thinks of money, look at who he gave it to," is another gem often attributed to her. She didn't grow up with it; she was born Dorothy Rothschild but famously said, "We didn't know *those* Rothschilds." Her father was in the rag trade, making suits and cloaks in what is now SoHo. She didn't marry for money, either. In both of her unions, she earned more than her spouse did. When she had money, she spent it extravagantly on hats, fur coats, and expensive perfume. Mrs. Parker sailed to Europe in style, once booking passage on the grandest steamship of all, the French Line's *Normandie*. She might have enjoyed drinking a Millionaire—even if she never became one. Harry Craddock captured two different recipes for the Millionaire in his 1930 collection, *The Savoy Cocktail Book*. Be a multimillionaire and try both variations.

old-fashioned glass

MILLIONAIRE #1

1 ounce sloe gin
1 ounce apricot brandy
1 ounce Jamaica rum
Juice of 1 lime
1 dash grenadine

MILLIONAIRE #2

1½ ounces gin
1½ ounces absinthe
1 teaspoon triple sec
¼ teaspoon grenadine
1 egg white

FOR THE FIRST VERSION, SHAKE ALL INGREDIENTS OVER ICE;
STRAIN INTO A CHILLED COCKTAIL GLASS.

FOR THE SECOND VERSION, VIGOROUSLY SHAKE ALL INGREDIENTS OVER CRACKED ICE.
STRAIN INTO A CHILLED COCKTAIL GLASS OR AN OLD-FASHIONED GLASS FILLED WITH ICE CUBES.

Note: The original recipe for the second version called for absinthe, which can be difficult to find. You can substitute with Pernod or another anise-flavored liqueur. Another variation substitutes bourbon for the gin.

Mint Julep

A FRIEND OF THE ALGONQUIN ROUND TABLE BUT NEVER A MEMBER, AUTHOR AND newspaperman Irvin S. Cobb boisterously commanded the American literary scene for two generations. H. L. Mencken compared him to Mark Twain, and Cobb's sixty books were best sellers. Born and raised in Paducah, Kentucky, Cobb was so admired that in his lifetime a hotel and bridge were named for him. (The hotel is long gone, but the 1929 span from Paducah across the Ohio River to Brookport, Illinois, is still in use.) A Louisville distillery tapped the humorist in 1936 to produce *Irvin S. Cobb's Own Recipe Book*. In it he waxed

poetic about his home state's most famous mixed drink: the Julep. He explores its Kentucky creation as carefully as a heart surgeon explaining how to operate on a patient. "So great has been the argument on this subject that often the controversy could only be solved by recourse to pistols at dawn," Cobb wrote, and he believed that the addition of nutmeg prompted Kentucky to join the Civil War: "It was brought on by some Yankee coming down South and putting nutmeg in the Julep. So our folks just up and left the Union flat."

Writing of the mint he put in his julep, Irvin S. Cobb said, "Like a woman's heart it gives its sweetest aroma when bruised." ◆ ◆ ◆

old-fashioned
glass

12 sprigs fresh mint
Powdered sugar
3 ounces Kentucky whiskey

PLACE 10 MINT SPRIGS IN A BOWL, COVER THEM WITH POWDERED SUGAR AND JUST ENOUGH WATER
TO DISSOLVE THE SUGAR, AND CRUSH WITH A WOODEN PESTLE. POUR HALF THE CRUSHED MINT
AND LIQUID INTO AN OLD-FASHIONED GLASS OR IN A STERLING SILVER OR LEAD-FREE PEWTER
TANKARD. FILL GLASS HALF FULL OF FINELY CRUSHED ICE. ADD THE REST OF THE CRUSHED MINT
AND LIQUID AND FILL REMAINDER OF THE GLASS WITH CRUSHED ICE. ADD WHISKEY TO THE BRIM.
REFRIGERATE FOR AT LEAST 1 HOUR—BUT IDEALLY 2 OR 3 HOURS IF YOU CAN WAIT THAT LONG.
DUST REMAINING SPRIGS OF MINT WITH POWDERED SUGAR, PLACE AS GARNISH, AND SERVE.

Note: According to Cobb, "The majority of Kentuckians, the folk of Chicago, the middle and far
west, Texans, Missourians and Louisianans swear by holy Bourbon, but all the deft technicians,
wheresoever found, agree that the liquor must be old, mellow whiskey—the blandest in its
savor, the richest in its perfume, the most lingering in its softly-expiring after-aroma."

◆ ◆ ◆

One group holds that the bruised mint should be left in
the potion. But my grandfather always insisted that a
man who would let the crushed leaves and the mangled
stemlets steep in the finished decoration would put
scorpions in a baby's bed.

—Irvin S. Cobb's Own Recipe Book

Monkey Gland

It's an understatement to say that Dorothy Parker disliked flappers, sheiks, and youth culture. "I hate the Younger Set. They harden my arteries," she wrote in one of her hymns of hate.

> There are the Male Flappers;
> The Usual Dancing Men.
> They can drink one straight Orange Pekoe after another,
> And you'd never know that they had had a thing.
> Four débutante parties a night is bogie for them,
> And their talk is very small indeed.

In the Jazz Age many adults suddenly acted like teenagers, and one of the legacies of that shift is a cocktail with an odorous name that hints at a gruesome practice. In the 1920s, Harry MacElhone, proprietor of Harry's New York Bar in Paris, took note of the spirit of the age and named this drink for a Russian nutcase, Serge Voronoff, who infamously transplanted tissue from the sexual organs of monkeys into humans to slow the aging process. This is the recipe used in London's Café Royal and Hotel Savoy in the 1920s.

cocktail glass

1½ ounces dry gin
1½ ounces fresh orange juice
3 dashes absinthe
3 dashes grenadine

SHAKE ALL INGREDIENTS AND STRAIN INTO A CHILLED COCKTAIL GLASS.

Note: If you can't find absinthe, substitute Pernod or Bénédictine, a Cognac-based liqueur from Normandy.

A young woman models flapper fashion from head to toe in 1922. ◆ ◆ ◆

New York Cocktail

Many exult E. B. White's 1950 paean to Gotham, Here Is New York, as the ultimate love letter to the city. But "My Hometown," a long-overlooked article by Dorothy Parker published in *McCall's* in 1928, is equally moving and touching. It's also the best statement Mrs. Parker ever wrote about why she loved the city. In fewer than one thousand words she masterfully distills its majesty. The New York Cocktail was a favorite in speakeasies that served rye and bourbon. This recipe dates from 1930.

old-fashioned
glass

2 ounces rye whiskey or bourbon
¾ ounce fresh lime or lemon juice
2 dashes grenadine
1 teaspoon powdered sugar
Orange peel

SHAKE LIQUID INGREDIENTS AND SUGAR OVER CRACKED ICE, STRAIN INTO A
CHILLED OLD-FASHIONED GLASS, AND GARNISH WITH AN ORANGE TWIST.

London is satisfied, Paris is resigned, but New York is always hopeful. Always it believes that something particularly good is about to come off, and it must hurry to meet it. There is excitement running in its streets. Each day, as you go out, you feel the little nervous quiver that is yours when you sit in a theater just before the curtain rises. Other places may give you a sweet and soothing sense of level; but in New York there is always the feeling of "Something's going to happen." It isn't peace. But, you know, you do get used to peace, and so quickly. And you never get used to New York.

—Dorothy Parker, "My Hometown," 1928

Old-Fashioned

IN DOROTHY PARKER'S OSCAR-NOMINATED SCREENPLAY FOR *SMASH-UP* (1947), cowritten with Frank Cavett, former gin joint chanteuse Angelica Evans (played by Susan Hayward) announces: "I'm going to have a little drink. Make me something . . . Come on, we'll both have one. An Old-Fashioned. Only no sugar, no vegetables, and go light on the ice. Why corrupt good liquor?" The Old-Fashioned is one of the oldest of all American cocktails, and it has earned its name by being more than 200 years old. This whiskey cocktail has been reinterpreted many times, but this is the traditional recipe from the speakeasy era.

old-fashioned
glass

1 sugar cube or 2 teaspoons simple syrup
1–2 dashes Angostura bitters
1 teaspoon water
2 ounces whiskey
Lemon peel
Orange slice
Maraschino cherry

IN AN OLD-FASHIONED GLASS, MUDDLE THE SUGAR CUBE OR SIMPLE SYRUP, BITTERS, AND WATER UNTIL SUGAR DISSOLVES (IF USING A CUBE). FILL GLASS WITH ICE CUBES AND STIR IN WHISKEY AND LEMON TWIST WITH A SPOON. GARNISH WITH THE ORANGE SLICE AND CHERRY.

Susan Hayward received an Academy Award nomination for Best Actress for her role as an alcoholic lounge singer in *Smash-Up: The Story of a Woman*. Dorothy Parker was also nominated for the screenplay. ◆ ◆ ◆

Orange Blossom

Robert Benchley was Dorothy Parker's best friend and a charter member of the Vicious Circle. He was also a teetotaler who made it through four years at Harvard and then seven years in newspaper and magazine publishing before touching a drop of alcohol. Benchley then fell into the bottle and never emerged. Along with Mrs. Parker and fellow writers Donald Ogden Stewart and Marc Connelly, Benchley frequented Tony's, a speakeasy on West Forty-ninth Street. Proprietor Tony Soma, formerly of the Hotel Knickerbocker, liked to stand on his head to delight customers. The story goes that a Tony's bartender once asked Mrs. Parker what she was having. "Not much fun," came her quick reply. Benchley didn't start drinking until his thirties. "The first social drink he took was an Orange Blossom," his son, Nathaniel, recounted in a biography of his father. "He tried one sip, then put the glass down and looked around the room, 'This place ought to be closed by law,' he said and everybody fell off their chairs with laughter." This recipe for an Orange Blossom comes from the Robert Benchley Society.

cocktail glass

1 ounce gin
1 ounce fresh orange juice
1 teaspoon powdered sugar
Orange peel

SHAKE GIN, ORANGE JUICE, AND SUGAR OVER ICE; STRAIN INTO A COCKTAIL GLASS.
GARNISH WITH FLAMED ORANGE PEEL.

Note: This cocktail has also been called an Adirondack Special, because of the homemade gin made in the region, as well as the Florida, due to the orange juice.

This "old-wives" super-
stition that a cup of
black coffee will "put
you on your feet" with a
hangover is either pro-
paganda by the coffee
people or the work of
dilettante drinkers who
get giddy on cooking-
sherry. A man with a
real hangover is in no
mood to be told "Just
take a cup of black cof-
fee" or "The thing for

A 1912 graduate of Harvard, Robert
Benchley wrote for magazines and
newspapers before becoming a radio
and motion picture star. ◆ ◆ ◆

you is a couple of Aspirin." A real hangover is
nothing to try out family remedies on. The only
cure for a real hangover is death.

—Robert Benchley, *My Ten Years in a
Quandary and How They Grew* (1936)

Ray Hitchcocktail

FOR FIVE SOLID YEARS, FROM 1918 TO 1923, DOROTHY PARKER WROTE THEATER criticism for *Vanity Fair* and *Ainslee's*. The Hotel Wallick in Times Square named a drink for one of her favorite stage comedians, Raymond Hitchcock, who appeared in shows with W. C. Fields, Fanny Brice, and Mary Eaton. He toured with the *Ziegfeld Follies* before moving into silent films, and Mrs. Parker always gave him a glowing review. In 1918 he was in a show called *Hitchy-Koo*, about which Mrs. Parker wrote,

> *No matter what the show may be, if Raymond Hitchcock is in it, it's a success. He runs at top form from the moment he clubbily makes his appearance in the orchestra, welcoming the incoming audience, to the final thud of the curtain . . . Miss Ray Dooley gathers in a large share of the laughs of the evening, particularly in one delicate scene where she plays an obstreperous baby whom Mr. Hitchcock, as the proud father, silences with a blackjack . . . even though I do wear shell-rimmed glasses on occasion; there is always something about a gentleman hitting a lady over the head with a stuffed club that causes me to rock with happy laughter.*

A clever bartender honored Raymond Hitchcock with the cleverly named Ray Hitchcocktail, so remember Old Broadway with this one.

cocktail glass

1 pineapple slice
Juice of half an orange
2 ounces sweet vermouth
Dash Angostura orange bitters

IN A SHAKER, MUDDLE THE PINEAPPLE AND ORANGE JUICE. ADD THE VERMOUTH.
SHAKE WELL WITH CRACKED ICE AND STRAIN INTO A COCKTAIL GLASS. ADD DASH OF BITTERS.

Raymond Hitchcock was a star on Broadway and in silent pictures. ◆ ◆ ◆

The Rob Roy was invented here, the old Waldorf-Astoria Hotel. Demolition started in October 1929 and lasted twelve weeks. The 16,000 truckloads of debris were dumped in the ocean off Sandy Hook, New Jersey. The Empire State Building rose in its place. ◆ ◆ ◆

Rob Roy

THE HERALD SQUARE THEATRE, A 1,300-SEAT PLAYHOUSE ON THE CORNER OF Broadway and West Thirty-fifth Street, opened in 1883 and showcased musicals and light operas for a quarter century. In 1894 *Rob Roy* opened there, based on the life of Scottish outlaw and folk hero Rob Roy MacGregor. With music composed by Reginald De Koven and a book by Harry B. Smith, it was a smash success. The *New York Times* called the operetta "clean, frank, manly, bright, and winsome" and praised star William Pruette. At the time, the old Waldorf Hotel—its bar and restaurant a famous destination for well-heeled theatergoers—lay just a short walk east, where the Empire State Building stands today. Bartenders at the hotel honored the cast and show by naming a Scotch cocktail for the production. The Herald Square was converted to the city's first movie theater in 1911. The theater was razed four years later and the hotel demolished in 1930, but the Rob Roy has thrived for more than a century. Try one on November 30, St. Andrew's Day. This recipe appeared in the 1937 *Café Royal Cocktail Book*.

cocktail glass

2½ ounces Scotch
¾ ounce sweet vermouth
¾ ounce dry vermouth
3 dashes Angostura bitters
Maraschino cherry

SHAKE THE SCOTCH, BOTH VERMOUTHS, AND BITTERS OVER CRACKED ICE.
STRAIN INTO A CHILLED COCKTAIL GLASS AND GARNISH WITH THE CHERRY.

Seersucker Punch

The Velveteen Rabbit, Las Vegas

LAS VEGAS NEVER HOSTED DOROTHY PARKER AT ITS GAMING TABLES, BUT SHE DID LOVE playing card games. A bridge fiend, she wrote about that game often, and other members of the Round Table were degenerate poker players: Heywood Broun lost his house at the table, and Harold Ross was gutted of $30,000 in one night. In that spirit, we turn to Bryn Esplin, creative director at The Velveteen Rabbit, a lounge in the Las Vegas Arts District. She created Seersucker Punch. "The word originates from the Persian *shir o shekar,* meaning 'milk and sugar,' probably from the resemblance of its smooth and rough stripes to the smooth texture of milk and the bumpy texture of sugar," Esplin said in *Zelda* magazine.

When it was first introduced in the United States, the seersucker suit was considered to be a poor man's suit. It wasn't until Princeton students in the 1920s, in an ironic fashion statement, began to wear the fabric, subverting the economic associations. Hollywood actors were spotted in seersucker suits, and Life *deemed it acceptable to wear in the northern part of the U.S. Writers would proudly wear it in beach settings, and dapper men made it their new go-to summer suit.*

Following its tradition of breaking boundaries, Seersucker Punch can be served either hot or cold.

lowball glass

1½ ounces bourbon
½ ounce Frangelico
½ ounce root liquor
1 teaspoon brown sugar simple syrup
½ ounce almond milk
Dash of cinnamon

STIR ALL THE LIQUID INGREDIENTS TOGETHER, POUR OVER SHAVED ICE IN A LOWBALL OR PUNCH GLASS, THEN ADD THE CINNAMON. TO SERVE THE PUNCH HOT, HEAT TO TASTE, STIR, AND TOP WITH A DASH OF CINNAMON.

Sidecar

THE LOST GENERATION THAT SWEPT INTO FRANCE FOLLOWING THE GREAT WAR included many American expats. Dorothy Parker joined them, making her first journey in 1926. There she befriended Gerald and Sara Murphy, while socializing with F. Scott Fitzgerald, John Dos Passos, and Ernest Hemingway. She did almost no work in Europe. Instead Mrs. Parker spent her vacations at luxury hotels, cafes, and—a world away from Long Branch—the beaches of the Côte d'Azur. Along with the French "75," the Sidecar also came back from World War I to America. Cocktail enthusiasts believe it was created in Paris at Harry's New York Bar for a regular customer—a military officer of some stripe—who was usually delivered to the establishment via motorcycle (with sidecar attached). It was popular during Prohibition but later lost its footing to new vodka and rum drinks. This recipe comes from the 1937 *Café Royal Cocktail Book* compiled by London bartender William Tarling.

cocktail glass

1 ounce brandy
¾ ounce Cointreau
¾ ounce fresh lemon juice

SHAKE ALL INGREDIENTS OVER CRUSHED ICE; STRAIN INTO A COCKTAIL GLASS.

Note: The Cointreau adds all the pop to this drink, so the brandy doesn't need to be an expensive or premium brand.

Reginald Vanderbilt was a millionaire dilettante who didn't accomplish much in his life except purchasing race cars and racehorses. He mixed Stingers for his friends in Newport and New York. ◆ ◆ ◆

Stinger

THE STINGER FIRST CAME INTO FASHION DURING THE GAY NINETIES FOR UPPER-CLASS New Yorkers, when the chief ingredient was always brandy. Cognac and other spirits were substituted later. It always had a reputation as a rich-person's cocktail and was the preferred drink of W. Somerset Maugham, the sophisticated English author and playwright who wrote a tender introduction to *The Portable Dorothy Parker* in 1944. The Stinger was also a favorite of railroad scion Reginald Vanderbilt (father of Gloria, grandfather of Anderson Cooper). Reggie Vanderbilt had a home bar and mixed his own Stingers every afternoon for friends. In the 1960s, Gloria Vanderbilt and her fourth husband, Wyatt Cooper, took Mrs. Parker under their wing; some of the last parties that Mrs. Parker attended were with the glamorous society couple—maybe having Stingers.

cocktail glass

2¼ ounces Cognac
¾ ounce white crème de menthe

STIR THE BRANDY AND CRÈME DE MENTHE WITH ICE;
STRAIN AND SERVE IN A CHILLED COCKTAIL GLASS.

Note: You can replace the cognac with brandy, gin, or bourbon—but *white* crème de menthe is key. If you order this drink, don't let the bartender reach for a bottle of the green stuff.

Stone Fence

Smash-Up EARNED TWO ACADEMY AWARD NOMINATIONS IN 1947: FOR BEST ACTRESS in a leading role, to Susan Hayward for playing a boozy nightclub singer, and for screenwriting team Dorothy Parker and Frank Cavett. The Stone Fence dates to the Colonial period and was made by farmers in the winter using hard cider. This is the most common recipe, which uses brandy, just like Angie drinks it onscreen, but substitutes apple cider for her rye.

old-fashioned
glass

2 ounces brandy
2 dashes Angostura bitters
½ ounce lemon juice
Club soda or fresh apple cider

POUR BRANDY AND BITTERS INTO A CHILLED OLD-FASHIONED GLASS FILLED WITH CRACKED ICE. ADD LEMON JUICE. TOP WITH CLUB SODA OR APPLE CIDER. STIR GENTLY.

Note: If you prefer, you can replace the brandy with applejack, bourbon, rum, rye, or Scotch, and the cider with club soda.

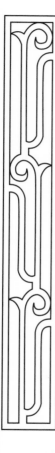

In one of the best scenes in *Smash-Up*, Susan Hayward's character, Angelica Evans, walks behind the bar in her Sutton Place apartment and grabs a bottle of brandy. The dialogue is pure Parker.

Angie: Hey, you know what a Stone Fence is? (*smiling*)

Mike: You mean a Stone Wall.

Angie: I mean a Stone Fence, brother. It's sort of like an ice cream soda, with conviction. Bartender, will you please get me a cocktail shaker with some shaved ice, and some brandy, and some whiskey, and some Cointreau? What you need, Mike, is a Stone Fence. Just about the most colossal drink you've ever drunk. Drank. It puts poise in apathetic people, if you know what I mean. And after the second one your spine turns to solid platinum. You take one part brandy and two parts rye . . . (*she drinks a jigger of rye*).

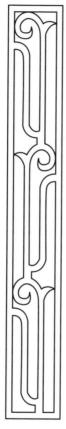

Sure Shot

Death & Company, New York City

THE MARTINEZ OF THE 1880s WAS SUPER SWEET AND CALLED FOR A WHOPPING amount of vermouth. It gradually morphed into today's Martini (depending on which history book you believe). In bars across the country, the fashion of reinventing classic drinks has taken hold. Hidden behind a heavy wooden door on Manhattan's Lower East Side you'll find Death & Company, a relative newcomer but a go-to spot for sampling updates to century-old cocktail recipes. "The Sure Shot is a classic Martinez variation," says Jillian Vose, head bartender. "The Martinez is one of my favorite drinks. When making it, I love using a split base of different Old Tom gins so that it isn't too sweet. So I thought, *Why not do a split with Old Tom and Genever?* I love me some Bols Genever! We were messing around doing a workshop for a bunch of Bols brands, and we had picked up a bunch of herbs and spices. Ancho chile was one of them, and it all spiraled to deliciousness from there."

Nick & Nora glass

1½ ounces Hayman's Old Tom Gin
½ ounce Bols Genever
¾ ounce Ancho Chile–Infused Dolin Rouge Vermouth
1 teaspoon Galliano Ristretto
½ teaspoon Demerara Syrup
1 dash orange bitters

POUR ALL THE INGREDIENTS INTO A MIXING CUP FILLED WITH ICE AND STIR.
STRAIN INTO A NICK & NORA GLASS. DO NOT GARNISH.

Note: If you can't find a Nick & Nora glass, use a cocktail glass instead.

A Guide to Speakeasy Slang

$\blacklozenge \quad \blacklozenge \quad \blacklozenge$

Speakeasy culture was born with the passage of the Eighteenth Amendment to the Constitution, and with it a whole new lexicon of slang sprang up. What has come down to us from that time forms a collection of English as colorful today as it was in 1920.

Anything very good was the *cat's pajamas*, the *cat's whiskers*, or the *bee's knees*. To be called *Four-O* was to get the highest possible rating from your friends. An *oil burner* was a gum-chewing girl. If you were from the country, you were a *Young Otis*; traveling salesmen and out-of-towners were the *Butter and Egg Man*. A young woman carried *mad money*, the cab fare in her purse in case she got into a row with her sweetheart. *Ritzy* also came into vogue courtesy of playwright George S. Kaufman in 1921 in the *New York Tribune*:

> *"The Crock of Gold"*
> *She's got a Hickson model walk*
> *And a line of Ritzy talk —*
> *Simple little Katie from old Ire-land*

A flapper who couldn't keep in the swim was a *dud*, a *Dumb Dora*, or a *dumb bunny*. A wallflower was a *sinker*; and, oh no, any flapper over thirty was deemed a *flat tire*. Guys who always picked up the tab were *darbs*; men who never went out with girls were tabbed *Red Mike*. A *cake eater* or *cakie* was self-indulgent and often decadent. A *cakie* who squired around a different girl every night was a *snake*.

If you were in the rumble seat of a 1926 Franklin Sport Coupe, you may have engaged in *snugglepupping*, which is the same as *petting* or *spooning*.

Robert E. Sherwood may have won the Pulitzer Prize four times, but he gave us a very important expression in a 1931 play: "I think it's time for me to announce that I'm not going to bed with you." Sherwood also gets credit for another famous two words: *indecent proposal*. Dorothy Parker—first to coin "what the hell?" and "ball of fire"—has three other great relationship phrases to her credit: "to mess around," "one-night stand," and "daisy chain."

The toast "Here's looking at you" came into vogue in 1928 in a book by Joseph March:

The drinks were placed,
Gus withdrew.
"Well—" said Tony:
"Here's lookin' at you!"

Drinkers carried *hip-flasks*. To be intoxicated was to be *jammed*, but *loaded* didn't mean drunk; it meant someone had good information. Getting *ossified* needs no explanation, nor does *to the gills*. For the first time, *hair of the dog*, an alcoholic drink taken to alleviate the effects of alcoholic drink, was on tap. Maybe that drink was *giggle-water*?

Bootleggers also used fantastic jargon. "On the slough" was what happened when the law found a speakeasy and the proprietors had to lie low for a few days. *Motherships* were vessels used to transport illegal booze from port to port; smaller tugs and watercraft then ferried the cases from the motherships to dry land. Crooks had nicknames for the law: a *harness bull* for a uniformed policeman, while plainclothes cops were *sleeves*. Detectives were *dicks* (possibly derivative from the London slang, *Richard*), and cops were *elbows*, as the *New York Times* reported in 1924, "Possibly because the elbow is prominent in the process of collaring."

Donald Ogden Stewart, an early member of the Algonquin Round Table, dreamed up one of the best phrases about a big night out: "To drink you under the table."

Illustrator John Held Jr., captured the spirit of the Roaring Twenties. ◆ ◆ ◆

A Helpful Guide
to 1920s Slang

and how: emphatic agreement
bee's knees: something extraordinary, the ultimate
beef: complaint
beeswax: business
bluenose: prude
breezer: convertible car
bum's rush: ejection from an establishment by force
cash: kiss
cat's meow: something splendid or stylish
dick: private investigator
ducky: very good
gams: woman's legs
giggle water: alcohol
glad rags: going-out clothes
hair of the dog: alcoholic hangover drink
joint: club, usually selling alcohol
pill: unlikable person
whoopee: good time

After we threw on our glad rags and hopped in the breezer, we found a joint with giggle water that was just ducky. We were minding our own beeswax, making whoopee, when some bluenose with beef—probably a dick—gave us the bum's rush! What a pill. Anyway, some hair of the dog would be the cat's meow. And how!

Three Miler

THIS DRINK, ALSO KNOWN AS THE THREE-MILE LIMIT, TOOK ITS NAME FROM THE DISTANCE offshore that bootleggers ferried hootch during Prohibition. It was believed the smugglers were in international waters—incorrectly as it happens. For the Coast Guard, though, this was serious business. In New York waters, cutters enforcing the Volstead Act fired on pleasure boats that then sank, occasionally with loss of life. Smugglers used motherships past the three-mile limit, then transferred the cases of liquor to smaller and faster boats. Two of the most popular products were rum and brandy, both used in this Prohibition-era recipe.

cocktail glass

1½ ounces Bacardi rum
¾ ounce brandy
1 teaspoon grenadine
1 dash fresh lemon juice
Lemon peel

SHAKE ALL LIQUID INGREDIENTS OVER ICE; STRAIN INTO A
COCKTAIL GLASS. DROP IN A LEMON TWIST.

◆ ◆ ◆

Times Square Cocktail

DOROTHY PARKER SPENT THE MAJORITY OF HER LIFE WITHIN STRIKING DISTANCE OF Times Square. Except when writing screenplays in Hollywood or making a brief stab at domestic life in Pennsylvania, Mrs. Parker was never more than a short taxi trip to the crossroads of the world: where Broadway, Forty-second Street, and Seventh Avenue converge. As a child she lived fewer than thirty blocks north and accompanied her father and sister to Broadway shows on a constant basis. Her years as a dramatic critic brought her to the Times Square theaters five and six nights a week. Her office jobs at *Vogue* and *Vanity Fair* were a block away, as were the offices of *The New Yorker,* her publishers, and the office she rented with Robert Benchley. Mrs. Parker hobnobbed at the Astor Grill atop the Hotel Astor (Forty-fifth Street) and laughed at the *Midnight Frolic* on the roof of the New Amsterdam Theatre (Forty-second Street).

But if she came back today, she wouldn't recognize Times Square. Since her death in 1967, soaring office towers have replaced all four corners of "The Deuce," most of the theaters have been razed, and nearly every former drinking establishment has become some chain restaurant or ho-hum retail space. The Times Square Cocktail evokes an era when streetcars were on Broadway—not costumed characters from Sesame Street.

wine glass

1½ ounces Southern Comfort
⅓ ounce sweet vermouth
½ ounce grenadine
Champagne
Orange wheel

SHAKE SOUTHERN COMFORT, VERMOUTH, AND GRENADINE OVER ICE.
STRAIN INTO AN ICE-FILLED WINE GLASS. ADD CHILLED CHAMPAGNE TO
THE BRIM AND STIR GENTLY. GARNISH WITH THE ORANGE WHEEL.

The *New York Times* gave Times Square its name; the former newspaper office is where the ball drops on New Year's Eve. ◆ ◆ ◆

Tippy Canoe

DOROTHY PARKER AND T. S. ELIOT BOTH WROTE POETRY IN THE 1920S, AND BOTH shared a bleak outlook on many subjects. The similarities end there. While Mrs. Parker sold her pieces to popular magazines, Eliot worked at an English bank. Mrs. Parker never penned a monumental poem, but in 1922 Eliot authored "The Waste Land," in which he wrote:

> At the violet hour, the evening hour that strives
> Homeward, and brings the sailor home from sea,
> The typist home at teatime, clears her breakfast, lights
> Her stove, and lays out food in tins.

A Chicago poetry fan plucked out "the violet hour" to christen a Wicker Park cocktail lounge, with a tip of a chilled glass to Eliot, born 300 miles away in St. Louis. The menu of The Violet Hour—known for its fresh juices, homemade syrups, in-house bitters, and a dedication to minimalist cocktails—changes seasonally, as does the façade of the building. One drink on the menu is the Tippy Canoe, "a riff on a classic daiquiri," according to bar manager Robert Haynes. "When working with fewer ingredients, balance is extremely important. Bonal is a French gentian and quinine-forward aperitif. This one is simple and accessible."

coupe glass

¾ ounce Smith & Cross Jamaica Rum
¾ ounce Bonal aperitif wine
¾ ounce apricot syrup
¾ ounce fresh lime juice
1 dash Angostura bitters
Lime wheel

COMBINE ALL LIQUID INGREDIENTS IN A SHAKER, ADD 5 ICE CUBES, AND SHAKE VIGOROUSLY. DOUBLE STRAIN INTO A COUPE GLASS AND GARNISH WITH THE LIME WHEEL.

Note: Fresh lime juice is a must. Also, The Violet Hour serves the
drink in a coupe, but you can use a cocktail glass.

How to Make Apricot Syrup the Chicago Way

According to Robby Haynes of The Violet Hour, making your
own apricot syrup is quick and easy. Take 13 ounces of apricot
preserves (such as Bonne Maman) and add four cups of granulated
sugar and one quart of warm water. Stir to incorporate. "A stick
mixer or handheld will make your life a little easier," Haynes
advises. "If not, a little elbow grease should do it." Strain through
cheesecloth. It will keep for two weeks.

The Windy City and the Vicious Circle

After New York City, Chicago has the strongest ties to the Algonquin
Round Table. The dean of the group, Franklin P. Adams, was born
there. The artist Neysa McMein attended art school in Chicago before
moving to Manhattan and launching a brilliant career. Poet John
V. A. Weaver, a native, worked for the *Chicago Daily News*, and it was
there that H. L. Mencken discovered him. Dorothy Parker's biggest
crush, the scoundrel Charles MacArthur, was a reporter for the City
News Bureau of Chicago. However, the biggest link to the city comes
via Edna Ferber, who penned Chicago's greatest novel, *So Big*, after
living there in the early 1920s. Ferber's timeless story of truck farmers
and the American dream won the Pulitzer Prize in 1925.

Tom and Jerry

During the Great Depression, Seagram's took out splashy two-page ads in mass-market magazines. It was no doubt a copywriter's dream account. "At the bar, at the club or at home—Be Sure of Finer Taste." Each ad included a half a dozen simple recipes for the company's gins and whiskies for the home bartender, and with each the company exhorted: "Think before you Drink . . . say Seagram's—and be sure!" This recipe ran in *Life* in 1937: "A fine warming drink for 'after the game.'" The Tom and Jerry takes its name from characters created by English writer Pierce Egan in *Life in London, or Days and Nights of Jerry Hawthorne and his elegant friend Corinthian Tom* (1823).

coffee mug

1 egg
1 tablespoon sugar
Dash of vanilla extract
2 ounces whiskey or rum
Hot water

SEPARATELY BEAT WHITE AND YOLK OF THE EGG, THEN GENTLY MIX
TOGETHER. STIR IN SUGAR AND VANILLA AND POUR MIXTURE INTO A COFFEE
MUG. ADD WHISKEY OR RUM, THEN FILL WITH HOT WATER.

Note: The original recipe called for brandy.

Tom Collins

THE CONVOLUTED HISTORY OF THIS DRINK DATES TO NINETEENTH-CENTURY LONDON. Returning doughboys brought their love of the Tom Collins back from Paris in 1918, and, with gin becoming one of the main bootleg liquors of Prohibition, the easy-to-make Tom Collins caught on. The drink was originally called a John Collins and appeared in Jerry Thomas's 1876 bartending guide. Served in a big glass, this "gin punch" proved popular at speakeasies, lawn parties, and summer resorts.

collins glass

Juice of 1 lemon
1 teaspoon powdered sugar
1½ ounces gin
Club soda
Maraschino cherry

IN A TALL 16-OUNCE COLLINS GLASS, PLACE 3 OR 4 ICE CUBES. POUR IN
THE LEMON JUICE AND SUGAR, ADD THE GIN, THEN FILL TO THE TOP WITH
COLD CLUB SODA. STIR AND GARNISH WITH THE CHERRY.

Note: Replacing the gin with another potable changes the name of the drink: Pedro Collins (rum), Mike Collins (Irish whiskey), John Collins (bourbon). A Mojito is also a variation: Substitute good light rum for the gin and the juice of a lime instead of a lemon. Garnish with sprigs of mint.

Twentieth Century

YOU CAN CAPTURE THE ROMANCE OF A PREWAR RAILROAD JOURNEY IN A GLASS WHEN you mix up a Twentieth Century cocktail, named for the New York Central Railroad service between Manhattan and Chicago. Passengers traveled in luxury Pullman cars—rolling drawing rooms, bedrooms, compartments, dining cars, lounges—for the sixteen-hour trip. In 1938 the Twentieth Century Limited locomotives debuted a streamlined Art Deco look in two shades of gray with aluminum and blue stripes. Traveling those thousand miles made for a luxurious adventure lost on us today. (You can get a feeling for it, though, in Alfred Hitchcock's *North by Northwest*.) Trainspotting author and gourmand Lucius Beebe adored the Twentieth Century Limited, writing that he "slept the sleep of the unjust, awash with Hennessy Three Star and Upmann Coronas." This cocktail replaces his beloved Cognac with gin and a French twist.

cocktail glass

1½ ounces gin
¾ ounce Lillet Blanc
½ ounce white crème de cacao
¾ ounce fresh lemon juice
Lemon peel

SHAKE LIQUID INGREDIENTS OVER ICE FOR 20 SECONDS, STRAIN INTO
A CHILLED COCKTAIL GLASS, AND GARNISH WITH A LEMON TWIST.

Note: Lillet Blanc is the key ingredient for this cocktail. A French aperitif,
it should always be served chilled, never warmer than 46°F.

To celebrate the centenary of Grand Central Terminal, the 20th Century Limited returned to New York in 2013. ◆ ◆ ◆

Ward 8

Dorothy Parker and her friends had a rocky relationship with Boston, Massachusetts. Mrs. Parker's only arrest happened there in 1927, when she was protesting the planned execution of accused anarchists Nicola Sacco and Bartolomeo Vanzetti. Robert Benchley was born and raised in Worcester, forty-five miles away, and graduated from Harvard, across the Charles in Cambridge. Fellow Round Tablers Robert E. Sherwood and Heywood Broun were also at Harvard.

One of the city's finest cocktails also originated there. A variation on the classic whiskey sour, it was a natural shoo-in for the rye-loving Vicious Circle. Its history begins at the Locke-Ober restaurant in the Hub. Bartender Tom Hussion concocted the drink in 1898 to celebrate an Election Day victory by Democrat Martin Michael Lomasney, boss from the Eighth Ward, who was running for state office. As fate cruelly had it, though, Lomasney later supported Prohibition, and the Locke-Ober suffered. The restaurant reopened and thrived for many years before being shuttered again for good. The Ward 8 lives on, though, as Boston's most famous cocktail export.

cocktail glass

2 ounces rye whiskey or bourbon
½ ounce fresh lemon juice
½ ounce fresh orange juice
1 teaspoon grenadine
Maraschino cherry

SHAKE ALL LIQUID INGREDIENTS OVER CRACKED ICE, STRAIN INTO
A COCKTAIL GLASS, AND GARNISH WITH THE CHERRY.

Whiskey Sour

Magazine writer Joe Bryan claims that Dorothy Parker requested a dear little one of these—one of her avowed favorites—for breakfast. Drinks guru David Wondrich credits the popularity of this drink, an all-American cocktail that predates the Civil War, to being simple and flexible. "From roughly the 1860s to the 1960s," he says, "the Sour, particularly its whiskey incarnation, was one of the cardinal points of American drinking and, along with the Highball, one of the few drinks that could come near to slugging it out with the vast and aggressive tribe of cocktails in terms of day-in, day-out popularity." This recipe comes from a 1936 whiskey drinks guide published by Frankford Distilleries in Louisville, Kentucky.

sour glass

1½ ounces American blended whiskey
½ teaspoon powdered sugar
Juice of half a lemon
Seltzer
Slice of orange, pineapple stick, or red cherry (garnish)

SHAKE WHISKEY, SUGAR, AND LEMON JUICE OVER CRACKED ICE; STRAIN INTO A SOUR GLASS. ADD A LITTLE SELTZER WATER AND DECORATE WITH FRUIT IF DESIRED.

Will Rogers

ONE OF THE BIGGEST BROADWAY STARS OF THE PRE–
World War I era was a laconic cowboy from
Oklahoma. Will Rogers got his start onstage in
1912 at the Victoria Theatre in a Wild West show,
delivering dry comedy lines alongside lariat tricks.
Florenz Ziegfeld initially disliked having a cowboy
in his refined productions, but the well-oiled
crowd loved Rogers's gentle barbs at rich people
in the audience. Rogers starred in the *Midnight
Frolic* on the New Amsterdam rooftop shows and
became a national star when he moved into the
Follies. In a 1918 review, Dorothy Parker wrote,
"The life of the evening is Will Rogers, who, to me,

Will Rogers in *Handy Andy*
(1935). ◆ ◆ ◆

is one of the Greatest Living Americans." Rogers went on to become a radio and
movie star and a beloved newspaper columnist in hundreds of newspapers—
until he died with friend Wiley Post, who crashed their plane into an Alaskan lake.
The Oklahoma Hall of Fame honors both men, and both have airports named
after them, but of the two we drink only to Will Rogers.

cocktail glass

1½ ounces gin
½ ounce dry vermouth
½ ounce fresh orange juice
1½ teaspoons triple sec

SHAKE ALL INGREDIENTS OVER ICE; STRAIN INTO A CHILLED COCKTAIL GLASS.

◆　◆　◆

Communism is like prohibition, it's a good idea but it
won't work.

—*The Autobiography of Will Rogers*

Yale Cocktail

DOROTHY ROTHSCHILD NEVER MADE IT PAST THE TENTH GRADE, BUT SHE TALKED HERSELF into the Ivy League in a manner of speaking. One of her most notorious quips—which she denied ever uttering—followed her to the grave and is particularly loathed around New Haven. Alexander Woollcott, in the "Our Mrs. Parker" chapter of *While Rome Burns*, recounts "that wholesale libel on a Yale prom. If all the girls attending it were laid end to end, Mrs. Parker said, she wouldn't be at all surprised." In 1924 she wrote, "I hate College Boys; They get under my feet," adding:

> *They list all the débutantes*
> *In Grades A, B, and C,*
> *And proceed accordingly.*
> *Once they get into their stride,*
> *The Opposite Sex hasn't a prayer.*

During World War I, bartender Hugo R. Ensslin collected the Yale Cocktail into his slim collection of drink recipes.

cocktail glass

2 ounces dry gin
1 ounce French vermouth
1 teaspoon maraschino liqueur
1 tablespoon simple syrup
3 dashes orange bitters

STIR ALL INGREDIENTS IN A MIXING GLASS WITH CRACKED ICE; STRAIN INTO A CHILLED COCKTAIL GLASS.

Note: Other Ivy League recipes of the era are the Harvard Cocktail (brandy and bitters) and the Princeton Cocktail (a dry Martini with two dashes of lime juice).

Ziegfeld

FLORENZ ZIEGFELD STILL RANKS AMONG THE MOST BRILLIANT SHOWMEN TO LIGHT UP Broadway. His productions glamorized American women, as no one else had, in glittering musicals that were the toast of the town for twenty-five years. His career began in 1893 in Chicago, before he went to Europe, where he found vaudeville acts to import back to America. He launched the *Follies* in 1907, and it became an annual institution at the New Amsterdam Theatre. Stars of the *Follies* became known as the most dazzling women in Manhattan. Dorothy Parker asked, "Where the Ziegfeld girls come from will always be one of the world's great mysteries; certainly, one never sees any like them anywhere around." The show launched scores of major names, including Fanny Brice, Eddie Cantor, W. C. Fields, Mary Pickford, Will Rogers, Sophie Tucker, and Mae West. Ziegfeld's widow, Billie Burke, one of the most famous actresses of the 1920s, contributed this recipe to the *Stork Club Bar Book* in 1946.

cocktail glass

2 ounces gin
1 ounce fresh pineapple juice
¼ ounce simple syrup
Pineapple slice

SHAKE LIQUID INGREDIENTS OVER HALF A CUP OF ICE CUBES; STRAIN INTO A CHILLED COCKTAIL GLASS. GARNISH WITH THE PINEAPPLE SLICE.

Note: The original recipe for this cocktail didn't include simple syrup but was probably made with sweetened pineapple juice. Simple syrup is also known as pure cane sugar syrup and open kettle molasses and has about sixty calories per tablespoon.

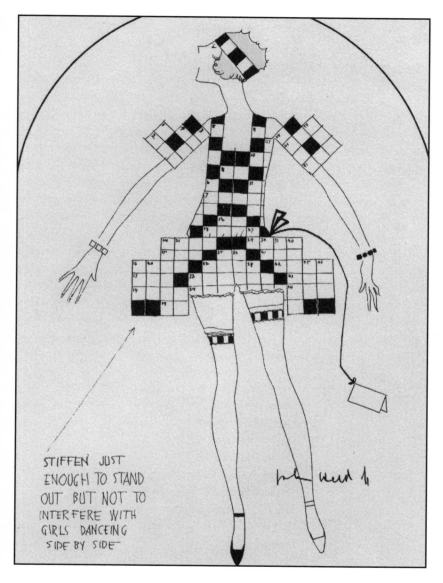

STIFFEN JUST
ENOUGH TO STAND
OUT BUT NOT TO
INTERFERE WITH
GIRLS DANCEING
SIDE BY SIDE

A costume sketch by the great John Held Jr., for the Follies includes instructions for the designer. Invented in Italy in 1890, crosswords became a big fad in the 1920s. ◆ ◆ ◆

Zombie

THE 1939 WORLD'S FAIR IN FLUSHING MEADOWS, QUEENS, WAS A SENSATION. WITH "Building the World of Tomorrow" as its theme, the fair pushed the premise that science and technology could provide economic prosperity and personal freedom. The fair also offered a ray of hope between two of the darkest events in the nation's history: the Great Depression and World War II. The fairgrounds stretched 3.5 miles long and in some places a mile wide, hosting approximately 26 million people the first season. To convey its message, the fair used icons, symbols, demonstrations and, best of all, exhibitions. *The Trylon and the Perisphere*—a 700-foot-tall spire and globe as large as a city block—became the fair's focal point and instant symbols of the machine age. The must-see Futurama exhibit at the General Motors pavilion presented a 36,000-square-foot model of a future America in 1960. Of the many theme restaurants, shops, and pavilions, the Hurricane Bar stood out by serving this drink. "Why people drink them I don't know," according to Vic Bergeron (aka Trader Vic). "Personally, I think they are too damn strong." Donn Beach of Hollywood's Don the Beachcomber fame (and who also invented the tiki bar) created the most beloved version of the Zombie. It's a lot of work to make—and exceptionally potent.

collins glass

1 ounce white rum
1 ounce golden rum
1 ounce dark rum
151-proof rum
½ ounce brandy (apple, cherry, or apricot)
¾ ounce fresh pineapple juice
¾ ounce fresh papaya juice
Juice of 1 lime
Pineapple slice

IN A SHAKER FILLED WITH CRACKED ICE, SHAKE ALL LIQUID INGREDIENTS EXCEPT
THE 151-PROOF RUM. STRAIN INTO A COLLINS GLASS FILLED WITH CRUSHED ICE,
FLOAT A SPOONFUL OF 151 ON TOP, AND GARNISH WITH THE PINEAPPLE SLICE.

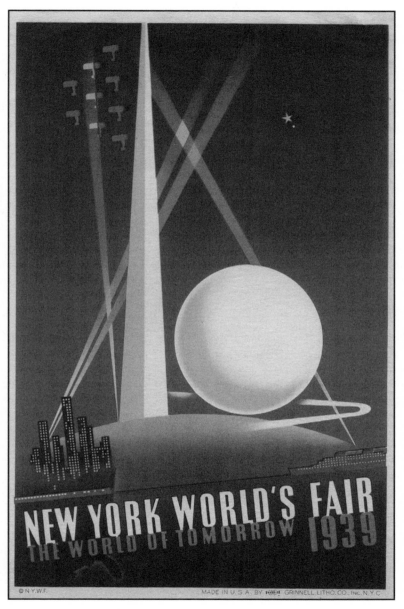

NEW YORK WORLD'S FAIR
THE WORLD OF TOMORROW 1939

The World's Fair of 1939–40 was one of the biggest events in New York City history. ◆ ◆ ◆

Photo and Illustration Credits

Author's collection: xii, 5, 17, 22, 27, 29, 41, 54, 59, 61, 71, 73, 84, 91, 93, 107, 120, 123

Photos by the author: 7, 15, 128

Don Spiro (donspiro.com): pp. xv–xvi

Shutterstock.com: pp. xvii–xviii

Public domain: p. 19

Courtesy of Joan Grossman, Susan Cotton, and Nancy Arcaro: Cablegram, p. 25

US Library of Congress, Prints and Photographs Division: pp. 32, 34, 37, 45, 47, 48, 63, 77, 87, 95, 96, 100, 111, 125

Vincent Gong, p. 117

Devon Quinn (author photo), p. 140

Design images licensed by Shutterstock.com.

Acknowledgments

This book came together as easily as a Russian nesting doll for many reasons. To start off, I thank the friends I've met and made through the Dorothy Parker Society (DPS). When a few of us got together over drinks on Dorothy Parker's birthday in 1999, I had no idea I'd be running the busiest literary society in New York all these years later. As I often say, we're a drinking club with a book problem, and we've had monumental tabs at some of the finest drinking establishments in the city. Through the DPS, I met Diane Naegel and Don Spiro. They started Wit's End, a monthly party to celebrate vintage cocktails, hot jazz, and period attire. It was through them that I started drinking many of the recipes in this book. Don says they launched Wit's End because they wanted to go to a party like it, and after five years the fun continues. The DPS doesn't have meetings, it has parties, and the ones with Wit's End are always the greatest.

I started the research for parts of the book more than ten years ago while writing the walking tours of the former haunts of Dorothy Parker and the Algonquin Round Table. This book gives me a chance to share with a larger audience a lot of the knowledge that I usually only impart as I walk backward in Times Square or the Upper West Side. I thank the Dorothy Parker researchers who went before me: Randall Calhoun (*Dorothy Parker a Bio-Bibliography*), Marion Meade (*Dorothy Parker: What Fresh Hell Is This?*), and Stuart Y. Silverstein (*Not Much Fun: The Lost Poems of Dorothy Parker*). Stuart's extensive notes on Mrs. Parker's life proved particularly helpful. In addition, the staff of the Algonquin Hotel, led by general manager Gary Budge, has always been supportive and taken a keen interest in the history of the hotel. Mr. Budge really does carry on the tradition of Frank Case, and it's a privilege for me to bring people to New York's best literary landmark.

For contributing modern-day speakeasy-style recipes, thanks go to: Alice de Almeida (Algonquin Hotel), H. Joseph Ehrmann (Elixir), Bryn Esplin (The Velveteen Rabbit), Chris Hannah (Arnaud's French 75), Robby Haynes (The Violet Hour), Barbara Jacobs (The Edison), Joanna Leban (Doc Holliday's Saloon), Kevin Martin (Eastern Standard Kitchen & Drinks), Hervé Rousseau (Flûte), and Jillian Vose (Death &

Company). My goal is to visit each of the establishments I've not yet been to and have these bartenders serve me these drinks in person. I can't wait!

If I could thank and acknowledge all of my favorite bartenders in New York, my publisher would need to add many extra pages to this book. These are a few who are special to me, and whom I'll never forget for the great times we've shared together: Andrew Bennetch, Mark Evangelista, Michele Gascoigne, Adam Gerston, Tracy Helsing, Timmy Hever, Chaundra Hugel, Carmit Israeli, Sara Walter, and Laurieanne Williams. Thanks for all the buybacks.

Two people who have had a huge influence on my love of cocktails are my parents, Don and Val Fitzpatrick. I'll never forget watching them order Martinis in a cozy pub in Tipperary, Ireland. They were handed tiny glasses of vermouth—while I had a fantastic pint of Guinness. My parents have had a Martini at six o'clock for most of their fifty years of marriage; on trips my mother packs her own Tanqueray, and it's my father's job to find the ice. At a family wedding one October, I ordered a gin and tonic, much to my mother's chagrin. "That's a summer drink," she sniffed. Ever since, I've had whiskey highballs after Labor Day.

Extra-special thanks to Christina, who supported me during the production of the book. My wife kept our rambunctious two-year-old busy as I plugged away measuring ounces and teaspoons of liquor. Christina is always supportive of my (numerous) side projects.

Big thanks to my editor, James Jayo, and all the good people at Lyons Press. The first time I met James, I put an Aviation in his hand, and we toasted to the success of this book. Thanks also to Allen Katz for writing the wonderful foreword. Allen gets my everlasting gratitude for naming a product after Mrs. Parker, and I believe the New York Distilling Company will get Dorothy Parker American Gin into all fifty states!

Sterling silver jiggers the author's parents have put to great use for forty years. ◆ ◆ ◆

Finally, I want to thank the legions of Dorothy Parker fans who take her to heart. You keep reading her stories and poems, producing shows based on her work, even recording your own music set to her words. The way to sustain an author's popularity after his or her death is to keep that legacy strong. Mrs. Parker now has a cocktail guidebook to go on the bookshelf with the biographies and collections of her work. Hopefully this book will draw even more new fans to learn about Mrs. Parker and lead some of them to her books.

Further Reading

Books

Benchley, Nat and Kevin Fitzpatrick. *The Lost Algonquin Round Table*. New York: Donald Books, 2009.

Chirico, Rob. *Field Guide to Cocktails*. Philadelphia: Quirk Books, 2005.

Craddock, Harry. *The Savoy Cocktail Book*. London: Pavilion Books, 1930, 2011.

Fitzpatrick, Kevin. *A Journey into Dorothy Parker's New York*. Berkeley, CA: Roaring Forties Press, 2013.

Meade, Marion. *Dorothy Parker: What Fresh Hell Is This?* New York: Penguin Books, 2007.

Parker, Dorothy. *Complete Stories*. New York: Penguin Classics, 2002.

———. *Complete Poems*. New York: Penguin Classics, 2009.

——— and Kevin Fitzpatrick. *Dorothy Parker: Complete Broadway 1918–1923*. New York: Donald Books, 2014.

——— and Stuart Silverstein (editor). *Not Much Fun: The Lost Poems of Dorothy Parker*. New York: Scribner, 1996.

Tarling, W. J. *The Café Royal Cocktail Book*. London: Pall Mall, 1937.

Waggoner, Susan, and Robert Markel. *Vintage Cocktails*. New York: Stewart, Tabori & Chang, 2000.

Wondrich, David. *Imbibe!* New York: Perigree, 2007.

Websites

The Dorothy Parker Society: DorothyParker.com

The Algonquin Round Table: AlgonquinRoundTable.org

The Museum of the American Cocktail, New Orleans: MuseumOfTheAmericanCocktail.org

Savoy Stomp: SavoyStomp.com

Tales of the Cocktail: TalesOfTheCocktail.com

General Index

Index by Main Ingredient

Index by Category

Old Favorites

Angel's Tit, 8
Between the Sheets, 16
Gibson, 49
Gimlet, 50
Gin Fizz, 51
Gin Rickey, 52
Highball, 58
Manhattan Cocktail, 69
Martini, 72
Mint Julep, 84
Old-Fashioned, 90
Rob Roy, 97
Sidecar, 99
Stinger, 101
Stone Fence, 102
Tom Collins, 115
Tom and Jerry, 114
Whiskey Sour, 119
Zombie, 124

Vintage Cocktails

Algonquin Cocktail, 6
Aviation, 12
Bailey, 13
Bathtub Gin, 14
Blood and Sand, 18
Boulevard, 20
Bulldog, 22
Bronx, 21
Cablegram, 24
Chicago, 26
Cuba Libre, 32
Death in the Afternoon, 33
Dubonnet Cocktail, 38

El Presidente, 39
Florodora, 43
French "75", 44
Horse's Neck, 59
Jack Rose, 60
Knickerbocker Cocktail, 63
Last Word, 64
Loud Speaker, 65
Love Cocktail, 66
Metropolitan, 82
Millionaire, 83
Monkey Gland, 86
New York Cocktail, 88
Orange Blossom, 92
Three Miler, 109
Times Square Cocktail, 110
Twentieth Century, 116
Ward 8, 118
Yale Cocktail, 121

Celebrity Cocktails

Alexander, 4
Josephine Baker, 62
Dempsey, 35
Dolores, 36
Jean Harlow, 61
Hemingway Daiquiri, 57
Ray Hitchcocktail, 94
Acerbic Mrs. Parker, 3
Mary Pickford, 76
Will Rogers, 120
Mamie Taylor, 68
Gene Tunney, 46
Ziegfeld, 122

Modern Classics

About the Author

Kevin C. Fitzpatrick is an independent historian who founded the Dorothy Parker Society in 1999. He is a graduate of Northeast Missouri State University and served in the U.S. Marine Corps. After his hitch he entered journalism and worked in newspapers, magazines, advertising agencies, and television in New York. He is a licensed New York City sightseeing guide and gives walking tours of city landmarks, literary sites,  watering holes, cemeteries, and unusual locations. Fitzpatrick frequently is a guest speaker at libraries, salons, and private clubs. In his spare time, he enjoys genealogy, collecting comic books, and dedicating bronze plaques for dead people. He and his family divide their time between the Upper West Side and Shelter Island.

Allen Katz is cofounder and vice president of the New York Distilling Company, which makes Dorothy Parker American Gin. The director of spirits education and mixology for Southern Wine & Spirits of New York, he also hosts *The Cocktail Hour*, a weekly program on Martha Stewart's SiriusXM channel. A past chairman of Slow Food USA, he serves on the board of directors for the New Orleans Culinary & Culture Preservation Society and the Manhattan Cocktail Classic, an annual four-day, four-borough celebration of the intersection between cocktails and culture. He and his family live in New York City.